The Labyrinth Effect:

The Many Faces of Answered Prayer

By JanMarie Sajna

Copyright © 2015
By JanMarie Sajna

All Rights Reserved.
This book, or parts thereof,
may not be reproduced in any form
without permission from the author.

First Paperback Edition 2015

ISBN-13: 978-1517166496
ISBN-10: 1517166497

Edited separately
by Cay Randall-May and Megan Hinman
Published by Create Space

Acknowledgements

Because this book is so much my story, it was at times very painful to write. If it weren't for my friends constantly encouraging me to continue, assuring me the story needed to be shared, I would never have been able to finish. So many dear people held my hand through this process, finishing the reading of one chapter and demanding the next before I even knew what it would be about.

My thanks to all my reader-friends who encouraged me to keep writing whenever I got bogged down: Bob Nunley, my Aunt Nona Engberg, Stephanie Bland, Sandra Mikulich, Cay Randall May, my sister Renee Driscoll, my mother Freddie Pitner, my brother Rory Pitner, my A.R.E. Search for God study group: Nanci Thomsen, Pam Enloe, Joy Rose, & Nancy MacClellan, my minister Erin McCabe & Evans Chigounis, Jerri Huggins, Ahria, and Mary Roseman … without you I could not have done it. Grateful appreciation goes to Jan Easton, my Australian friend who contributed many of her excellent photos of Findhorn. Jan, your photos are so much better than mine. So much gratitude to my son Adam Sajna whose computer expertise and photography skills helped me immensely, solving problem after problem in navigating anything to do with my computer. Thank you also, Adam, for the cover photo, and thank you John Gilluly and Grace Kohan for helping me design the cover. Special thanks to my editors, Cay Randall-May who did the first editing, and to Megan Hinman who did the final editing.

When this book was finished, I asked all those who had been reading bits and pieces of it over the years to help come up with the right title. As always, my friends came through with their many wonderful suggestions. One of my first readers did not respond to my request right away which surprised me. When I next saw her, she told me she had taken my request into prayer and wanted to tell me in person what happened.

"After praying every day for over a week, I was awakened in the middle of the night from a dream" Mary Roseman explained. "Someone appeared to me in the dream and told me that the name of JanMarie's book was The Labyrinth Effect."

Immediately I knew it was the right title. To me, this was a sign that those on the other side also felt the book was important and needed to be published so I finally quit procrastinating … and here it is.

Thanks would not be complete without acknowledging all the wonderful friends, acquaintances, and family who graciously allowed me to tell their story. I do not presume to claim I know how, why, or what they felt about what happened. I have tried to only report their stories as told to me, or as I experienced them. I love each of you, and do hope I gave your story the justice, the magic, and the telling it deserves.

My Thanks and Blessings to you all.

JanMarie Sajna

Contents

Introduction

Part I   **Praying**

Chapter 1   In The Beginning   1

Chapter 2   The First Visitor   11

Chapter 3   The Rest of the Week   19

Chapter 4   The First Miracles   27

Chapter 5   More Prayers Answered   35

Chapter 6   John   41

Chapter 7   Labyrinth Walkers   47

Part 2   **Traveling**

Chapter 8   Being Called   61

Chapter 9   First Week at Findhorn   69

Chapter 10   Programme Friends {Or Roses with Thorns}   77

Chapter 11   Findhorn Sanctuary   83

Chapter 12   Saint Germain   91

Chapter 13   Essence of the Arts   99

Chapter 14   Pottery   107

Chapter 15	Music	115
Chapter 16	Conception	123
Chapter 17	Christmas Miracles	135
Chapter 18	Findhorn Puzzles	147
Part Three	**Back in the USA**	
Chapter 19	Ahria and Angels	159
Chapter 20	Mt. Shasta	169
Chapter 21	What does It All Mean?	177
Chapter 22	And Other Odd Blessings	185
Part Four	**A New Journey**	
	Introduction	194
Chapter 23	Sell the House?	197
Chapter 24	Holos University	207
Chapter 25	Healing Past Lives	213
Chapter 26	Answers	221
Chapter 27	Why?	231
Chapter 28	Every Thought Is a Prayer	241

Foreword

JanMarie Sajna wrote about the many faces of answered prayer as a draft of a project she is working on in lieu of a dissertation at Holos University. She pulls together her experiences in a way that invites the reader to walk with her on her journey. She presents her studies in such a way that the reader can easily feel some of the ways she felt. That was especially true when she described the labyrinth she built in her front lawn in Independence, Missouri.

Hoping that the book would inspire people to embark on their own journey of prayer, the things that were most compelling to her were: how she learned to recognize the answers to prayer prayed in the Labyrinth; how the Labyrinth seemed to help her see those answers in new ways; how it helped her find clarity; how she was able to make connections, recognizing the synchronicity of events over a long period of time; and how it brought her to the people and places where the most amazing healings occurred!

Her goal is to help people learn how to pray and how to recognize answers to prayer in all its myriad faces. With that is also her intent to guide people in acknowledging their worthiness in receiving answers to prayer—and that is so much of what Affirmative Prayer is all about. She succeeded magnificently.

Reading this book will definitely improve your own journey of prayer. Be well and be in Joy.

Bob Nunley Phd
ISSSEEM Wisdom Council - Founding Chair
Holos University Graduate Seminary
Admissions Director and Professor

Introduction

This is the story of how I came to build a Walking Prayer Labyrinth in my front yard and my healing journey since its construction. As all journeys go, it took me places that seemed inaccessible ... places in the past, places in me, places in the lives of others, and places where amazing experiences and healings happened, and are still happening.

There are many books - scholarly books - about Walking Prayer Labyrinths. Some have a few personal stories, but most are more about historical data, ways to build labyrinths, and uses for labyrinths. My purpose in telling my story is not to teach you how to build a labyrinth, nor is it a history book or a book of instructions.

This is my story of how this labyrinth in my front yard changed my life. It perhaps changed also the lives of all whom I have met or who have walked it since its inception, and I share these stories because they may help someone in their own journey. I hope to inspire those who need healing to take a chance on beginning their own odyssey.

Though some of these events may be called miracles, I believe, though often extraordinary, that these experiences can happen to anyone. It's just a matter of being a searcher, open and trusting ... all while still retaining a healthy discernment coupled with common sense.

I have tried to write this story as it happened, as I learned how to pray, and how to recognize answers to prayer. Many times, past life this and that - both in this lifetime and others - had to be faced, so it may seem as though the story skips around. Please persevere, for it all does come together in the end.

Part One

Praying

ONE

In the Beginning

I went to the concert to listen to harp music. It was October 7, 2001.

A woman billed as the Crystal Harpist was scheduled to perform at the church I was attending that year, All Souls Unitarian Universalist of Kansas City. Bored and finding retirement odd, I went ... just for something to do. The music was wonderful, and the woman, gentle and peaceful.

At the end of the concert, the audience was invited to stay to walk a labyrinth that was being unrolled at the back of the sanctuary. The large piece of canvas with a design imprinted upon it was about 30 feet in diameter. I hung around out of curiosity and ignorance, as I had no idea what this labyrinth thing was all about. The Crystal Harpist began to give us some background about the history of walking prayer labyrinths and how there was a resurgence of interest in these ancient metaphors of life. She told us how these walking patterns seemed to be helping people to pray, to meditate, and to find answer to prayer.

She invited the adults to sit in a circle around the canvas labyrinth laid out on the floor. The lights in the room were dimmed, to make a meditative atmosphere yet not so much as to impair visibility. She told us the children would walk the labyrinth first. Then she laughed and said, "They will run it, for that is what children do."

She also told us to just watch them and to be open to whatever happened. One epiphany after another shone brightly for me while the children ran the labyrinth.

I found that if I just watched the kids running through the labyrinth, they all looked to be in a chaos that would have them careening into one another. But they weren't. My first epiphany was to recognize that what looked like chaos was actually each child following the path. It was the path that directed their footsteps. If I was able to focus on their feet, their foundation, I could see the path, but if I only focused on the individual child without seeing their path, I found myself judging how far they were from the center, from the goal.

I decided to follow one child's progress, focusing on her and then her feet. The pathway led the child I watched close to the center and I thought, "Ah, she's almost there!" but then the path led her back out toward the outer rim. My judgment of her progress was wrong. And the first metaphor of life, (Epiphany #1) smacked me between the eyes as I realized how often I judged the progress of myself and others when I had no clue as to what their or my path actually was. I was stunned in a way I'd never been before. The visual of this child's progress was something I had never considered in my self-righteous judgments about progress, whether mine or that of others.

The path of the labyrinth was narrow, so with about 20 children running it, there were often bottle-necks. Laughing, the children would wrap their arms around each other and baby step their way past. They did this with giggling and friendship, and they did it whether they were passing someone who wanted to go slower or whether they were meeting someone going in the opposite direction.

Epiphany #2: How easy it was for them to hug one another as they maneuvered around each other. They hugged with laughter and caring, and then let go and moved on.

"In life, how many of us do that? How often do I do that?" I asked myself. Either we demand someone get out of our way, or we hold on, not letting either them or us move on. "Why not hug in friendship and joy instead and help each other to make the transition?"

Epiphany #3 Then, I noticed that sometimes, the children ran along beside each other for short distances as sections of the path ran side by side, before each path would turn and go in an opposite direction, onto a different tier. Some of the children grasped hands and skipped along for those short distances, then hugged across path lines, let go and went on their way. And in this metaphor of life, I saw how hard so many of us hold onto one another instead of simply recognizing and accepting that the pathway has changed, and it is time to let go and again move on. I saw how hard it is for us to see that letting go is the right thing to do.

I asked myself, "How did I get stuck in the idea that once I have been with someone for awhile that I *have* to stay with that one person forever when it is, in reality, the time to turn away and go on?" Meeting someone doesn't have to deter me from my path, but it does enhance with joy those few moments as hands are held in support and fun for that part of the journey. It also bespeaks the need to be able to recognize where I am on a path, so as to not make commitments lightly or without consideration of each other's pathways. Maybe that's what's meant in the Bible about not yoking yourself to someone whose foundation, whose pathway is different than yours ... as well as on a completely different level of principle, values, spirituality, maturity, goals, etc.

The last of the children exited the labyrinth, and the adults were invited to walk.

We were so serious, all trying to be humbly prayerful and meditative. Me, too. I was in the middle of the group as we entered the labyrinth one by one. No one passed me, but I was uncomfortable with the slow pace set by the woman in front of me. She was really into her experience in a different way than I was, and I felt guilty at feeling restrained from my own natural rhythm.

Then I remembered how the children did it. So I moved up behind her, put my hand gently on her shoulder and whispered that I would like to pass. She smiled and turned to acknowledge my request. We put our arms around each other, laughing quietly and hugging as we baby-stepped our way around until I was in front of her. Smiling, we released each other, and I turned and went on in my comfortable rhythm. I realized that it wasn't a race, and we both knew it so we were quite peaceful with this adjustment.

As I came closer to reaching the center of the labyrinth, people had started on their way out, so now I had to pass those going in the opposite direction. Some just scooted by without touching. Somehow, you know which ones are going to do that; the no-eye-contact face and standing as close to the side of the path as possible gives it away. I respected their desire for no contact, and I inched past them. Others, with eyes full of smiles, rejoiced in the hugging baby-step scooting process around each other, and Epiphany #4 shook me. "Why be afraid of strangers? Why avoid each other? Why not open my arms and welcome the hug? Why let shyness, fear, or whatever, keep me from that experience?"

Epiphany #5 came in complete harmony with #4: "Why take it personally when someone prefers to hold themselves aloof? Why judge someone as shy or withdrawn when perhaps their place on the path was simply one of solitude, hence worthy of honorable privacy of space, body, and emotions?" I questioned. When it was my turn to step out of the labyrinth, my heart was light, and my smile was huge.

My prayer upon entering the labyrinth was simple. As I said, my retirement felt odd, leaving me with little to do, not much direction, and I was bewildered. My life as a teacher had for years included many extra avenues of education such as being the Public Relations Chair for the NEA teachers for the state of Missouri, editing a prize winning Newsletter, creating new curriculum to integrate the Fine Arts into the regular teacher's classroom, and extra responsibilities associated with the National Education Association, lots of committee work concerning various education legislative issues, as well as conducting storytelling workshops and performances. My time had been filled with much to do and to accomplish; hence this retired life was quite a change.

One huge recognition was that my social life had so strongly revolved around my career and committee work that I had no real connections, friendships, or social interactions outside of my work. Retirement was showing me a loneliness I didn't know I had. So my thoughts had been wondering if I should sell my house and move on … somewhere.

When I stood at the entrance to the labyrinth, I had mentally placed my house in one hand, and in the other hand carried the idea of selling my house and moving.

As I walked the labyrinth, my house which I had imagined being in my hand became brighter and brighter as if someone was turning the lights on inside of it - enough to make it seem to glow magically, a transformation I was not consciously controlling. The idea of moving became darker and darker until it faded away. When I reached the threshold of the labyrinth, I felt strongly that I was to stay in my home.

As I drove home, I could think only of this marvelous experience. Going to bed, I fell asleep so sweetly in a state of profound gratitude. I awoke early the next morning with the surety that I had to create a labyrinth in my own yard.

For the next week, I planned, measured, gathered supplies, designed ... and created a labyrinth in my front yard: A seven-tier labyrinth - in the Santa Rosa Style - 50 feet in diameter, and sandwiched between my driveway and a flowering dogwood tree.

Santa Rosa Labyrinth Design

The path was to be the width of my electric mower, and the lines were to be the width of a 9 inch paint roller. I drew the labyrinth on graph paper, including the path and line measurements to fit the parameters I'd chosen. One of my abilities which has served me well, is to figure out how to do something on paper first, then in actuality.

My next step was to wander around my garage, my basement, my shed, and my kitchen just looking at things and thinking. When I found the red masking tape and the long rope, somehow I just *saw* how to do it.

Gathering all my materials, I headed to the front yard where the first step was to hammer a smooth broom handle into the ground in the place which would become the very center of my labyrinth. I tied one end of a long rope to the broomstick, loose enough so it would slide easily as I walked in a circle around it. I measured off where each line of the Labyrinth would be on the rope and attached the red tape at each of those points.

The tape on the rope looked something like this when I was done:

8_____I_I_____I_I_____I_I____ ….

The 8 represents the center pole, and the I_I represents where a tier line (nine inches wide) would be located, and the space between the tier lines I_____I being the width of my electric mower.

Silly me, I didn't know they made spray paint that pointed down, so I painted the lines on the grass with a paint roller and some old blue house paint that I wasn't going to use. Holding the paint roller at the tier lines marked on the rope was not easy. I had to keep the line taut and the roller straight so it made a circle as I went. Attach two pencils with a length of string, I_____I and then try to make an accurate circle and you will see what I mean. Then imagine doing it with a broomstick, a rope, and a paint roller.

Painting grass with a paint roller is a strange, rather goofy way to do it. Each stroke of the roller picks up as much grass as it paints. So, after rolling the paint-covered roller 6 to 10 inches, the grass has to be scraped or picked off. Oh joy! It took me three days to paint those lines which in totality measured nearly 1000 feet long. Folks driving by engaged my sense of humor about the whole thing; their yelling comments about me being the witch or alien who creates crop circles made my cheeks pink up quite brightly. I live on a fairly busy street, so the comments were frequent and to be expected, I guess. I would just laugh nervously, wave, and shake my head …. then pick off some more grass, dip the roller into the paint, and continue turning my grass blue in lines forming the circled tiers of my Labyrinth.

Somehow, there was just no question about doing this, creating this Labyrinth. I had to do it. That is just all there was to it. It was mine to do, no matter how difficult, silly, wasteful or whatever. I had no choice.

I love times like that, when doubt isn't draping me like a shroud, when certainty is like sunshine warming my heart. It was wonderful to be in such a place in my mind, body and spirit.

Because I wanted seating in the center of the Labyrinth for meditation, and not wanting to spend any money, I engaged my creative process, and began looking around my property for something to use. The winter before had taken down a pretty big tree in the back yard ... at the very back of the back yard. The tree trimmer cut it up, went home for dinner with my check in hand and never returned to remove the big logs. At the time, I was quite annoyed, asking, "Why did I have to get left with this mess?"

Fortunately, the once-considered-negligent tree trimmer had cut the logs all about the same size, which also happened to be just about right for sitting upon, even though some were a bit on a slant. Each chunk must have weighed half a ton - at least, it seemed that way. I rolled about eight of those logs close to 175 feet from the backyard to the front. Oh my aching back!

Grunting and almost cursing, I arranged them in a circle around the inner perimeter of the center of my labyrinth. When I stood back and looked at them, I proudly thought "Hmm, my own Stonehenge."

I was done. And I was tired .... But, oh, so satisfied. There was now a blue seven- tier Walking Prayer Labyrinth painted into the grass in my front yard, and all I had to do was to let the lines grow 6 to 8 inches and keep the pathway mowed as short as (according to my son) 'healthy for the grass' could be.

Affirmative Prayer for Purpose

God's will for me is always for my highest good. God loves and empowers me with peace and strength to overcome all challenges. The wisdom of God guides and inspires me to take right action and to see clearly what is mine to do in partnership with God. My faith in God allows me to see all the good in my life, joyfully providing the light which guides me to success and safety. My every need is abundantly met as I walk God's Path for me.[1]

---

[1] *The prayers at the end of each chapter are Affirmative prayers, a way of praying which I learned as a Silent Unity Prayer Chaplain. These prayers are sometimes paraphrased, sometimes whole sentences are taken directly from Silent Unity's prayer guide, and some I wrote myself.*

TWO

The First Visitor

A couple of weeks after completing my Labyrinth, I woke on a Saturday morning with that old "what do I do with myself" angst rearing its ugly head again. I got up pretty early - before daybreak - came downstairs, and booted up my computer while my coffee pot sang along.

I went to www.Realtor.com and began looking on-line at property around the country, wondering again if I should sell and move. How soon we forget! I was checking prices, wondering where I could afford to live. The hours went by. I took a break, got dressed, had a bite to eat and was back on the computer when the doorbell rang. It was about 1:00 in the afternoon.

A tall, attractive African-American lady stood at my door … in her forties, perhaps. She was staring intently at the Labyrinth with on odd expression on her face. When I opened the door, she spoke with the anxiety of needing to know. "What is that in your front yard?" She asked. "I have to know. I was driving by and suddenly saw it, so we turned around and came back. What is it?"

"It's a Walking Prayer Labyrinth." I told her. "It's for a kind of meditation and prayer that uses your whole body. It helps you to focus in your prayer."

Very agitated, she spoke again. "I think I have seen this in a vision." she said. "I'm not sure, but it looks like what I saw."

Because we were standing on the porch, we were only a few feet higher than the Labyrinth, so I asked her if it would help her to be able to see it in totality from the third floor of my house.

"Yes!" she exclaimed. "Would you mind?"

"Come in." I invited, and led her up to the third floor where we stood at the window looking down onto the Labyrinth. From there, the painted blue lines showed up very well, and the design could be seen quite clearly.

View from the third floor as Dorothy saw the Labyrinth

"I must tell you a story." The woman said. As we stood there, she told me her story - actually her *stories*, for there were three.

Her name, she told me, was Dorothy.

"First," Dorothy said, "I must tell you that the week I graduated from college, I was in a terrible car wreck. My chest was crushed, and I died several times. And several times, they brought me back. I didn't want to come back because the pain was so terrible, but Jesus appeared to me and told me that I had to return, that He had work for me to do. Since that time, I have had visions, many visions …."

Dorothy paused and gazed at the Labyrinth for a long time. Then she continued. "Seven years ago[2], I had just walked my son to the bus stop. I put him on the bus, and turned to go back to my house. Suddenly something appeared floating in the air above my mailbox. I saw glowing blue circles within circles within circles of light. I stared at it trying to figure out what I was seeing, and then I spoke aloud. 'Jesus. What is that?' I asked.

"Jesus stepped up next to me and answered, 'It is a magnetic field.'

"Slowly the blue circles within circles of light faded, as did the vision of Jesus, and I went back into my house," Dorothy concluded her first story.

---

[2] *The number of years bespeaks the synchronicity of what came next in Dorothy's story. Dorothy's seven years corresponded to the seven years before this event when I first saw my house in 1994. My niece, Glory, had accompanied me on a drive through the neighborhoods around Independence Square as I was showing her the area in which I was hoping to buy a house. There was one in particular that interested me, but upon finding that its price was way out of my league, I figured this neighborhood was just too expensive for me. We were heading east on Winner Road when I saw the house that I now own. I pointed it out to my niece and exclaimed, "It's a shame that house isn't for sale, as it's exactly what I want!" The house that I pointed out to my niece did not go up for sale until 3 years later.*

"Did what you saw look like what I have in my front yard?" I asked nervously. Piercing me with her stare, she nodded and just stood there looking at me for awhile as though trying to decide just what else she should tell me.

Dorothy then said. "The next vision I am to tell you about is this: Four years ago[3], I was standing at the window in my bedroom watching my children playing in the backyard when Jesus stepped up next to me and said. 'I want you to move to Independence, Missouri.'"

"I was born and raised in Texas," she told me. "I've never lived anywhere else, never really went anywhere else."

Dorothy continued, "I was astonished. I said., 'Independence, Missouri! I don't even know where that is! I've lived in Texas all my life …. My whole family is here!"

"Why do you want me to move to Independence, Missouri?'" Her voice echoed the tone I guessed she must have used that day, as it rose in incredulity.

---

[3] I bought my house four years previous (in 1997) to Dorothy's visit. The day my little patio house in Blue Springs sold, I decided I'd better get busy and find another home. I drove to the area where I'd first begun looking for a house, near Independence Square. It was a quiet Sunday, not much traffic, and I was happy to stop at an Open House. [The realtors were probably the oldest realtors still active in the business, Myron and Eleanor Hershey … in their early nineties and still sharp as ever.] Their Open House home was not what I wanted but upon describing my dream house to the Realtors, one said they had that house for sale but were not showing it because they were having trouble with the renters. When I drove by the address they gave me, I was astonished to find it was the very house I had pointed out to my niece three years previously. Because the house had issues, its price was within my range of possibility, so I bought it.

"Then Jesus took my hand," she smiled in remembrance. "And we moved up and out into space until we were looking down upon the earth. I saw that there was one large land mass, in the center of which was a glowing blue circular area of light. Jesus pointed to this glowing blue circle and said 'That is my Jerusalem. Now watch.'

"As I watched, the land mass began to break apart. Pieces began to float off. The area with the glowing blue circle of light split, and half of it floated off to the west. Gradually, the pieces of land began to take the shape of what I recognized as the continents. The glowing blue area moved farther to the west, and I saw land rise up out of the sea and encircle the blue piece. Then I saw that this new land had taken the shape of North America with the glowing blue area right in the middle."

Dorothy paused for a long while, and her eyes filled with tears as she remembered. "Then Jesus pointed to the blue area and said to me, 'That is my New Jerusalem, my Zion.' Then He turned and looked at me. 'That is Independence, Missouri.'"

"Immediately I was back in my bedroom, knowing without a doubt that I must move to Independence Missouri," Dorothy continued. "I packed up my children and my things, and we left only a day later. I have been here now for four years" (... *just as I had been in my house for four years.*)

Turning to me, Dorothy said, "This blue pattern in your yard, I saw in a vision. I don't know what it is for, but I do know that telling you these visions is what I was supposed to do. I don't know why... But I do know you were to be told." Then she turned and started down the stairs.

Not knowing what to say, what to think or even how to begin

processing this, I followed her back to my own front door.

I was bewildered ... fascinated, but unable to really grasp what she had told me. I didn't know whether to believe her. It was all so strange.

Dorothy went down the steps of the porch and stopped. She stood there for a moment with her head cocked to the side as though listening to someone or something. Then she turned and looked up at me and quietly reported, "Jesus said to tell you that you are not to move yet. He wants you to stay here for awhile longer."

The hair on the back of my neck stood up. I had not told anyone that I was thinking about moving. No one could possibly have known that I had been surfing the web looking at real estate around the country all morning. I stood there stunned as she got back into her car and backed out of my driveway. It was almost more than I could handle.

Genesis House front porch

Prayer for Spiritual Understanding

My heart and soul desires a closer walk with God. Through the power of the Christ within, I become aware of my spiritual nature. As I align myself with God ... to more fully experience the Presence, I gain insight into God's will for me, and insight in understanding the divine plan for my life. I am uplifted and inspired ... ready to experience the great and wonderful possibilities open to me now, for I know and have faith that God's love is constant and unconditional.

THREE

The Rest of the Week

Not sure how to process everything Dorothy had said, I tried to put it out of my mind and went about doing some chores. Of course, it was hovering there, barely kept out of sight and thought, for in a way, it was downright scary. "What have I created in my front yard?" was the question I was avoiding, while those very thoughts and questions pounded at my awareness.

Around 7 that Saturday evening, I prepared supper.

Now. I must backtrack slightly here. I am a very prolific reader, checking out four or five books each week and reading them all. My favorite dinner time pal is the stand upon which I prop my book to enjoy while I eat my meal. Living alone for many years leads to friends like books. That particular week when I had gone to the library, I did something rather out of character. Normally, I read book jackets carefully and even a couple of paragraphs before adding a book to my check-out stack. I find it such a waste of time to open a library book at home only to discover it holds no interest for me.

Unusually, only a few days previously, as I was walking up to the check-out desk at the library, I had noticed a paperback lying on one of the library tables. It had a picture on the front that was kind of glowing .... in shades of blue. Without even looking at the title of the book, I added it to my stack. It was taken home without any perusal of its subject or contents - highly unusual for me.

That Saturday evening I went to my stack of library books, and again without really looking at the book, I rather mindlessly chose the paperback to join me for dinner. Propping it open onto my book stand, I sat down to eat.

The prologue was a page and a half long. My fork dropped to my plate and my chin dropped to my chest. The hair at the base of my neck stood up like wee soldiers raising their bayonets to the sky, shivering in cold chills and strange energies.

The prologue was a description of how the one land mass on earth had split into the continents.

The book turned out to be a pretty good sci-fi story, but that prologue was almost more than I could absorb after my strange visitor that day. Knowing I needed to make some sense of this synchronicity, after dinner I decided to write an email to my quite logical son who was living in Boulder, Colorado about everything that had happened that day.

During the writing, I suddenly had what I can only describe as a waking vision. This vision was also a memory, a very strong memory that I put into the category of a vision because I saw and heard it so clearly while sitting at my desk that night, seemingly from out of nowhere, interrupting my writing.

A bit of background related to this vision: For more than a decade as a second grade teacher, my elementary classes would build a town on the floor of my classroom. Each year, this town was a big deal. It was once even written up as the cover story for the local newspaper. As part of this Social Studies Unit on Community, local leaders and utility folks in our town were invited to come to speak to my class about their roles in a town's life. Each year, one of my favorite visitors was a lady named Janet Conrow, who came from the Water Department with a great video and an interesting speech we all enjoyed.

My vision that Saturday in October was of Janet, standing in front of my class and our proudly built town on the floor. Sitting there at my computer that night, I heard her say as she had said so many times over the years to my various classes:

"Independence is very unusual, It sits upon one of the world's largest underground aquifers. We are floating." She would laugh then as the children's eyes grew big with the thought. "We are floating boys and girls - floating!"

Once again, my hair saluted my neck and this time the air puffed out of my lungs in a big whoosh.

After an anxious tossing and turning kind of night, the next morning I overslept and missed church (At this time, I was a member of All Souls Unitarian Church on the Plaza in Kansas City which is also where the Crystal Harpist shared her labyrinth.). So much hair standing-on-end sleep deprivation excitement had just worn me out. Around noon, my doorbell rang. A friend from church was at the door. It was the first time he'd ever come to visit, and I was surprised. He said he'd noticed my absence and had the thought that he should stop by to make sure I was okay. He actually lived in another town so 'stopping by' was a bit of a misnomer. No one had ever done this before or since when I'd missed church so this was odd.

When he asked, "Is something wrong?" I grabbed his arm, pulled him into the house, and replied, "Yes, come in … come in!"

We sat down with coffee, and I began immediately telling him about my Saturday's visitor, the library book, and water lady vision. I think I was hoping he could make some sense of it all, so my hair and my thoughts would calm down. He listened very carefully to my whole story, not looking at me, but gazing into his cup. Then he quietly smiled, and began to tell me about Independence Square.

First, he shared that he had grown up in this area, and asked if I knew very much about The Square. I didn't. I was born in Minnesota, raised partly on an island in the Puget Sound and partly in a log cabin in New Jersey, so what he had to tell me was *new*. He asked if I'd ever noticed how many churches were in the square mile around Independence Square. Shaking my head, he saw he needed to elaborate. He told me that many of the churches were actually headquarters of religions, and that many of them believed that it was here that Jesus would return as promised.

My eyebrows reached for the sky. "Independence, Missouri?" I asked incredulously. His response was to speak of what the religious folks around here called this area: "Zion." I decided then and there to take a drive around the Square and start counting churches. (*Note: I quit counting at about 20 later that afternoon*). His advice to me was to stay open, to pray and to listen, and to just be okay with all that was happening.

He did calm me down somewhat, but I was still on alert, nervous, and even a bit scared.

Later that week, I actually had a date. I think it was a Thursday night, and we went to dinner and who knows where else. It was the only date I ever had with this fellow, and I don't remember where I met him or even his name. What was memorable was what he told me when I shared the story of what had happened the previous Saturday. Considering that I hadn't had a date for several years, getting hooked up with this man in the first place was not the only oddity.

He also, like my church friend, listened quietly while staring into his coffee as I shared all that had happened that week. I fully expected him to laugh and place me into a category of "CRAZY", but he didn't.

Basically he said: You don't know this about me, JanMarie, but I have my Master's Degree in Botany. I actually did my Master's Thesis on this area because it is so unusual. There are very strong indications that **three land masses** met here. Weather scientists, botanists, and geologists all have various theories about the effects of those 3 land masses. Some think the weather here is affected by this. I'm sure you've noticed how severe weather seems to split and go around us quite frequently. In my study, I found indications of plant life that originated in three separate land masses

I was convinced. The synchronicities were just too powerful to put aside what Dorothy had shared about her visions. But I was left with so many questions that I felt overwhelmed and knew that I needed to go slow and just be open to whatever came …. open, sensible, careful, and cautiously awed … while in my mind's eye, I saw myself throwing my hands up into the air in surrender to this mystery that had entered my life.

It was all a new beginning for me, heralding a mystery that

confounded me, yet held a promise of something incredibly special. In honor of this promise, of this new beginning, I decided to name my house and my Labyrinth. To find that name, I walked the Labyrinth and simply asked what it should be. Without any hesitation or thought, the name popped bright and shining into my mind:

"Genesis House and Genesis Walking Prayer Labyrinth."

Winter covered the Labyrinth in snow, and buried my log seats, so I added a Christmas Tree for the holiday

Prayer for Calm and Peace

One with God, I let nothing disturb the calm peace of my soul. I experience this unshakable kind of peace by becoming still and centering on the presence of God within me. As I repeat the affirmation: God and I are One, I begin to feel the peace that comes from knowing I am not alone, that God is always with me.

Prayer for Divine Order

There is a divine plan for good at work in my life and that plan is now unfolding. No matter what the situation, God is present in all persons and in all circumstances. I trust in God, knowing that whatever I do, wherever I go, God is the wisdom that guides me, the power that governs me, and the love that blesses me. I release my concerns and I continue to act in integrity, expressing the love of God in every thought I think, every word I speak, and every action I take. In this time of transformation, I create new beginnings, new energy, and I enjoy the journey of each new day.

FOUR

The First Miracles

Walking the Labyrinth frequently, I thought a lot about how to pray. I wondered what I should pray for, what words I should use, how I should go about listening for answers, and how to stay grounded and sane with all these synchronistic events, experiences, and information swirling around me. I finally just came back to the place of my own needs. What did I need?

I realized I was very lonely. I had bought this big property and house with the hopes that my family would want to come to visit. One person living in a three story house (four counting the basement) with a Carriage House in the back seemed excessive. So I wanted folks to visit. I began to pray about it in the Labyrinth.

In January of 2002, just three months after creating the Labyrinth I got a call from my niece, Wendy, who lived in Colorado at that time. She asked if she and her children could come to see me for Spring Break in early March. Excitedly, I exclaimed, "Yes, yes, yes!" As it turned out, not only did Wendy come with her four children, but her sister Audrey came down from Iowa with her six kids. My house was full, and I was delighted.

The children took to the Labyrinth like tongues to a lollipop.

We walked it every day, a minimum of twice a day ... sometimes with umbrellas in the rain and sleet, sometimes with candles in the starlight, but always with joy, singing, sometimes dancing, while enjoying deep wonderful joyous prayer.

Wendy's youngest child, Garrett, who was about three and a half, was such a little general. He would run the Labyrinth, and then stand on the logs exhorting us all to sing. "Jesus Loves Me" was his favorite song to lead.

On a particularly fine starry evening during that March Spring Break, we lit candles and went out to walk the Labyrinth before bedtime. Most of the children were already walking while the last few waited at the entrance to allow space between walkers, as was our custom. While we waited, a young woman came staggering down the sidewalk in front of the property. She stopped and watched us for awhile, wondering, I am sure, what in the world we were doing. Finally she asked in a drunken voice, (proving my thoughts concerning her condition) "Whatcha doin'?"

I answered quietly, telling her that we were walking in prayer. She watched for another minute, and then muttered. "God's been trying to git me, but I'm a mess ...." Then she looked at me, and shyly asked, "Kin I, kin I do it, too?"

"Yes," I replied, and knowing she would need help, I took her hand. One of the children took her other hand and we began slowly to lead her along the path. She began to cry. She cried all the way to the center. We sat her on a log, and the children put their arms around her. And I saw their lips moving as they prayed for her. After awhile, they began singing their favorite song just for her, changing the words slightly to "Jesus Loves You," and she sobbed and sobbed. Someone

asked her name, and she mumbled, "Rose." So the song changed again, this time to "Jesus Loves Rose."
When she was able, we helped her up and guided her along the pathway back to the entrance. When she stepped out of the Labyrinth, she turned to me and asked. "Can I come back? Can I walk it again?"

"Of course." I said. "Anytime and anytime. You are so welcome." I hugged her and she hugged me back, clinging for a moment. Then she tremulously smiled, turned and slowly walked on down the street. (*Unbeknownst to me then, I was to see Rose again, only a few months later.*)

Another evening of that week, we were out walking the Labyrinth when suddenly the smaller children began peering into the taller grass, which formed the lines of the Labyrinth. They began calling to me, "Aunt JanMarie, where is the blue light coming from? Do you see it? Where is it coming from?"

"Surely," I thought, "all the blue paint must be gone by now." As I searched in the grass, I saw that indeed the paint was gone. I was puzzled because I could not see anything that was blue.

The youngest children - the twins, Megan and Aubrey - and their little brother Garrett seemed able to see this blue light coming through the grass, which none of the rest of us could see. I had not yet told any of them about Dorothy's visit and what she had said to me about the glowing blue light Jesus had shown her in the vision by her mailbox and again as she floated above the earth watching the continents form. So this talk by the littlest children of a glowing blue light reminded me of that Saturday in October, and filled me with wonder ....
and also filled me with longing to be able to see this blue light

myself.

A morning toward the end of our week, on a sunny day, when we were all gathered in the center of the labyrinth and had prayed for everyone we could think of, I asked if anyone had someone or something else to pray about. Cherie Danielle, Wendy's oldest child, shyly raised her hand and asked, "Aunt JanMarie, is it okay to tell you about a dream I had this morning? It was so real. I thought it was real until I woke up and I was still in my pajamas and still in my bed." There was such a wonder in her voice and puzzlement about this dream that we were all captivated.

Immediately the goose bumps rose up on my arms, and knowing what she was describing could only be a vision, I encouraged her to continue. "I dreamed, I woke up just before sunrise in The Eagle's Nest.[4] It was really quiet, so I got up, got dressed and tiptoed down the stairs," Cherie Danielle began.

"I put on my coat, unlocked the front door, and went outside to walk the labyrinth. The sun was just coming up. I walked really slow and was praying. When I got to the middle, I stopped and looked up, and I saw Jesus standing over there under that tree." She pointed to the east at the tree in my neighbor's front yard. "He talked to me." Tears filled her eyes. "I can't remember what Jesus said, but I know He loves me, and I know I'm going to be okay."

At that moment, her little sister Megan stood up, and with her hands on her hips, exclaimed, "That's my dream! How did

---

[4] *The children all slept in the big open 30' by 17' room on the third floor. This was their space and they had made their beds in various corners of the room, some areas tented for privacy and fun. They named it The Eagle's Nest.*

you dream my dream? Except Jesus wasn't under that tree" and she pointed west to the tree on the southwest corner of my property. "He was under that tree over there, and he had those pokey things on his head." Still pointing to the tree at the front of my driveway opposite to Cherie Danielle's tree, she indignantly spouted as only competing siblings can, "He talked to me, too, but I don't remember what he said." She cried. "And He loves me too." Staring at her sister, she asked again, "How did you dream MY dream?"

Tears filling her eyes, Cherie Danielle took her little sister in her arms and just hugged her.

We were all stunned, but we were also all totally in belief that these little girls had indeed seen Jesus. Those moments sitting in the morning sun, all of us holding hands, eyes full of tears and hearts full of joy are some of the most precious moments of my life. We didn't know what to do or to say. We just felt that *love* that must have enveloped Cherie Danielle and Megan early that morning. Their story gave us what can only be described as a "huge hug" from Jesus.

Garrett, wonderful little Garrett, brought us back to the day when he hopped up onto his log seat, and standing there in his Little General stance, began to sing, raising his arms to conduct all of us in a resounding rendition of "Jesus Loves Me"

At the end of the week, everyone left, happy and peaceful … grateful for the time together … not knowing that Wendy's three daughters, Cherie, Megan, and Aubrey would be sustained with the love of Jesus in the months ahead as abrupt changes occurred in their lives

I recently found and developed a missing roll of film from that visit in March of 2002 of my nieces and nephews. The blue in the lines of labyrinth did not show up to our naked eyes, but in those photographs I was astonished to see that the camera was able to photograph the blue light.

Prayer for Children

The love and compassion that Jesus poured out upon the children still blesses them today. My faith is strong as I pray for _____. The Christ Spirit enfolds and surrounds _____ with soothing, healing energy, calming and giving confident awareness that the love of God is doing its perfect work in the life of _____. I believe in the power of prayer, and I rely on that power now as I pray for these children. Divine love works in and through all those caring for these children; the all powerful presence of God's love expressing through each care-giver and each child, and we all feel safe and secure.

Prayer for Divine Order

We turn within, knowing that there is no place where God is not, and God is absolute good. We trust in God, knowing that whatever we do, wherever we go, God is the wisdom that guides, the power that governs, the love that blesses, the presence that protects, and the substance that prospers us. As we move forward, this perfect order is established.

FIVE

More Prayers Answered

Various people began walking the labyrinth. I would see them sometimes through my front windows. Other times, I invited people to walk, and tried to be available for anyone with questions.

At that time, a young teacher was renting the apartment in the Carriage House on my property. Her gentleman friend, Miles, was very interested in Genesis Labyrinth, and I learned that he was walking it before going to work each morning, around 4:00 a.m.

One day, I complained to Miles that I wasn't getting answers to my prayers. I'd been praying to meet someone. A man. One just for me. I'd been single for 24 years and as I said, "Lonely!" So, I'd been praying about it. I had even found a little book about how to attract a man through prayer and intention. I'd made my list as recommended in the book. I think there were 17 items on the list of the kind of man I wanted. But I hadn't met anybody, let alone someone with the 17 listed attributes.

Miles and I were talking this day toward the end of April of 2002 as we stood at the entrance to the Labyrinth, and he was sharing how miracles seemed to be happening for him since he'd been walking the Labyrinth. He told me how he'd been trying to start a business but his biggest problems were finding the right artisans and the right suppliers. His specialty was rehabbing once fancy old houses ... mansions. The example he gave me about how answers were coming went something like this:

He said, "A few nights ago, I was standing in line at the grocery store, thinking about how I needed someone who knew how to remove, refurbish, and reinstall old Italian Marble. A woman was leaning on her cart behind me, half asleep." continued Miles. "It must have been around midnight. Before I knew it, my mouth opened and I exclaimed to her that I needed someone who knew how to work with antique Italian marble."

Miles laughed as he reported. "She blinked at me in surprise and with a very strong Italian accent, blurted out, 'My husband can do Italian Marble!'."

"That's how it happens," Miles finished. "It's like I keep meeting the people who know the answers or know someone who knows the answers, or I meet the suppliers themselves who have what I need ... like on some level, I am drawn to them and without any planning, my mouth just opens and I speak my need within their hearing. It's like one miracle after another."

"Wow!" I uttered ... jealously. "Why isn't that happening for me?"

"How do you pray?" Miles asked.

Like the good Catholic I had been raised to be, I clasped my hands at my breast, elbows tucked in, and lowered my head.

Miles laughed. "Look at you," he said. "You're all closed up. You don't have any room to receive. I pray like this!" He spread his arms out wide, with his palms up and his face open in joy to the sky. "I am open to receive," he repeated.

Miles, who is about 6'5" and weighs in like a linebacker, spread his arms out in joy and welcome for the answers.

"Oh!" Was my only response.

Later that night, in the moonlight, I went out to pray in the Labyrinth. Awkwardly at first, I spread my arms, opened my hands, and tried to find the place inside me to receive. And I encountered a fear inside of meeting someone. What if I wasn't good enough, pretty enough, sexy enough? What if I didn't know how to be in a relationship?

Somehow, I knew I had to let go of these fears and be open to receive. As I walked that night, it got easier and easier to let go the fears, and finally by the time I reached the center, I was feeling only a little nervous, the fear toning down to a barely discernible whisper. I laughed at myself, and felt the final puff of fear disintegrate ... a disintegration that lasted for a few minutes ... but must have lasted long enough to work.

The next day - a Friday -I headed out to Cargo Largo Recovery Sales Outlet to buy some sheet protectors to use for the resume I was sending out to various colleges applying for a teaching position in Storytelling. Once there, I headed for the office supply section of this huge warehouse store. They'd moved it, and I found that the aisles that used to contain office supplies now contained hunting supplies.

A young fellow was down on one knee, trying to stuff something back into its box. This thing seemed to be spring loaded and kept flinging itself out of the box. He was obviously getting frustrated. It was comical, and I stopped to laugh. He looked up at me and the most delightful grin spread across his face.

"What are you doing? What is that?" I asked.

"It's an elk decoy." He said, laughing. "And it won't get back into its box."

I saw some directions lying there, so I picked them up, looked at them, and knew I could help. Between the two of us, we finally got the elk decoy folded correctly and back into the box.

"Well" said this young man, "I guess you're just going to have to come elk hunting in New Mexico with me to help me handle this thing."

I laughed. I figured that he wasn't much older than my son. He seemed friendly but because his teasing invitation had befuddled me, I changed the subject. I asked him what he did when he wasn't elk hunting. He told me he was an artist. Because I am an artist, I was delighted and asked where he showed his work. When he replied that he didn't show his work anywhere, I began to tell him about a local gallery where I showed mine, a gallery at Blue Ridge Mall.

To make a long story short, John was not as young as he looked. He was only 10 years younger than me, and our relationship lasted more than seven years. I did go elk hunting in New Mexico with him, and it was one of the most amazing trips of my life.

And! He fit all 17 items on my list. John was an incredible

blessing for me. I learned so much from the relationship with him, a huge part of which was how to love and be loved. This was the first man I had met in all those years with whom I was really interested.

In oddly synchronistical events, we discovered that we had almost met several times over the years. We had bought our almost identical side by side refrigerators from the same store during the same week. I had done a storytelling performance at the school across the street from his house ... in a town a good 35 minutes from mine.

It took me a long time to realize that he also was built much like my father. His love of the outdoors, of woodworking, and of alcohol was also like my dad. And most of all, his hands, large and strong, were just like my father's.

Prayer for Love

The love of Christ fills my heart and I am a radiating center of divine love. I trust everything in my life to God's tender care, knowing that God's will for me is true happiness, soul enfoldment, and all that is good. The special love I have for others attracts to me those who share my interests and genuinely care about me. My heart responds with joy and gratitude. I attract a companion who expresses the attributes and qualities that I desire in a relationship, and I am fulfilled.

SIX

John

When John first came to my house in May of 2002, and saw the Walking Prayer Labyrinth, I had to explain it to him of course. John is very conservative and of the fundamentalist Christian persuasion in religion so my Labyrinth was a bit much for him to take.

As I told him some of the stories of the Labyrinth, I could tell he was doing his best to *not to roll his eyes.* His lips would twitch in the effort not to laugh. He was trying so hard to be seriously listening and respectful. Just as I was sharing about people actually coming to my door to tell me their stories, the doorbell rang.

A young woman stood there. It was Rose, the drunken girl who had walked with us over Spring Break. "I saw that you were home," she explained, "and I wanted to tell you what has happened in my life since I started walking your Labyrinth." I invited her in, marveling at how my words had suddenly come true just as I was speaking them. Talk about synchronicity! As John listened, I could see that the urge to roll his eyes and/or to laugh faded away as Rose told her story.

Rose shared with us that when she had come that first time the previous March, she had been homeless, on drugs, and spaced out most of the time. "I've been coming in the middle of the night to walk your Labyrinth." she said. "Sometimes, I even slept in it." Smiling nervously, she said, "I hope that's alright."

I nodded and she continued. "I didn't think I was good enough to be in a church, like I would make it dirty to be there. But here" and she gestured toward my front yard and the Labyrinth "Here it was okay. I could talk to God here." Pausing, she added shyly, "I'm the one who has been putting flowers in the birdbath in the middle." I had noticed that once in a while, there were dandelions or other wild blossoms in among the stones in my birdbath so I smiled in delighted recognition.

"Now," Rose said. "I am off drugs, I have a job and a place to live, and someday, I'm going to get my little girl back." She stood a little taller, and with a quiet pride, she added. "I was even arrested last week for an old warrant, but when I went to court, I didn't get crazy or anything. I just told the judge what I was doing, and that I needed to keep my job... so he didn't put me in jail and didn't even ask for bail. I was okay, and he could see that." She was so proud that the judge could recognize the change in her.

"I just wanted to thank you for having this Labyrinth here," Rose said, her eyes becoming teary. "Being able to pray here has saved me." I didn't know what to say. I hugged her in gratitude and joy, and she went on her way. Every so often I see Rose walking along the sidewalk on her way to and from her job. Once I even saw her with a little girl, and all the mowing in the hot summer days was suddenly so worthwhile.

When I found the Angel birdbath, it was John who set it up for me. Over the years, John had helped me find the stones and artifacts for the Angel birdbath. Even though he never prayed there and acted like he wasn't sure it was right, he did tell friends of his about it once in awhile. He also planted a tree in the center of the Labyrinth and coaxed it into a fine healthy addition to the beauty of the labyrinth.

John earns his living by throwing darts in tournaments. He is very good, one of the best in the state of Missouri. He often wins so everyone knows him, and he has quite a variety of friends and acquaintances. One night after a dart tournament, he told me that he'd been talking to a couple at the event who was interested in the Labyrinth. He asked if it was okay for them to come and talk with me about it.

"Of course" was my reply, and a date was set.

It was raining the night they came, and there were three - a married couple and her brother. The brother told us he was a mess, and he looked it. His sadness surrounded him like a great black cloak. It seemed he had been drinking a lot, and at times did illegal drugs. He'd lost his job, and his wife had kicked him out. He was distraught and knew he desperately needed help.

This was my first experience of ideas being spoken by me, which amazed even me. I found myself talking to this man with words of wisdom I didn't consciously know. As I listened to myself talking, I was listening like an audience myself to the words coming out of my mouth. He told me at the end of the evening that those words were exactly what he needed to hear.

I suspect that my daily walking meditation served to mold me into being a conduit for guidance for those who came for help. In later instances, I found that the words I spoke about walking prayer seemed to be extraordinarily suited to the particular listener. The gist of the message was always the same, but the approach changed as needed. This happened enough times that I knew the guidance was coming through me, not from me. I learned to listen to those words myself.

John never seemed very interested in the stories of the Labyrinth, but he did take care of it for me, often mowing and always trimming the lines, which required a weed eater I could not handle. He also moved more logs into the center.

After visiting for at least an hour with John's friends, when the time felt "right", we went out onto the porch. The man told me he didn't know how to pray, and he asked me to walk with and pray for him. I agreed and instructed him to walk in openness to receive. I suggested he walk with thoughts of gratitude for all he was receiving and to keep bringing his mind back to those positive ideas whenever negative thoughts drifted across his awareness.

We stepped out into the gentle rain, and I slowly led him through the Labyrinth. I began to pray. I knew this man was desperate for help, and my entire focus was to pray the best I could for him and to be the best possible conduit of prayer for him that I could be. I really wanted to help. I prayed.

And after awhile, I forgot about me. I forgot about the rain, my wet hair and damp clothing. I forgot about *me*! I forgot how long this was taking. I forgot about what a great person I was for doing this. And when all those egotistical thoughts were gone, I saw the blue light! But in my mind, my ego leapt up and exclaimed "THE BLUE LIGHT. I SEE THE BLUE LIGHT!" As soon as that part of me took over my awareness, the Blue Light disappeared. No matter how I tried, it did not come back. I was just too excited, my ego was too busy leaping for joy at how cool it was - how cool *I* was for being able to see that Blue Light.

My *ego* got in the way, and the adrenalin of the moment would not let me get back into the zone - the Blue Light Zone - where prayer resides. It reminds me of a paradoxical religious teaching which says how a truly humble man does not know he is humble, yet the second he notices he is humble, he is no longer humble.

It was to be another year or so before I saw the Blue Light again. It occurred with another of John's friends, a young man who had become my friend too. He was another man who was spending too much time in an alcoholic haze but who wanted to get his life under control. Again, my caring about him led me to walk in prayer with him after he said he didn't know how to pray.

Once again, my focus was so strong on praying for him that I saw the Blue Light. Once again, my ego leapt up and cried out "I see the Blue Light!" And once again, it disappeared.

Prayer for Healing

The Spirit of God dwells in you and you are filed with life-restoring energy. You release any troubled thought or feeling, and hold to your faith in the face of any challenge. As you give your attention to life-affirming ideas and true understanding that you are a beloved child of God, God's life and love flows within your mind and body as a steady stream of healing energy and strengthening power.

Prayer for Spiritual Understanding

My heart and soul desire a closer walk with God. Through the power of the Christ within, I become aware of my spiritual nature. My heart's desire to know of my oneness with God allows the inner Christ presence incredible power to change my thoughts and actions; I am enfolded in God's love and light. I know I am growing in love, wisdom and freedom. This assurance strengthens my faith and brings me peace.

Prayer for Others

God knows your needs and assures you that you are worthy and deserving of bountiful goodness. You turn, in trust, to God for the perfect fulfillment of your every need. The Holy Spirit moves in and through your life in powerful ways that harmonize your thoughts and feelings. Your peace of mind, freedom, prosperity, health, freedom from addictions, and success are assured. God's will for you is an abundance of all things necessary for a happy and success-filled life.

SEVEN

Labyrinth Walkers

The Angel birdbath began a new era for Genesis Labyrinth. With it placed at the first turn of the Labyrinth, walkers were greeted with crystals, colorful stones, and bits of ceramic, even carved bits of stone in its basin. At the entrance to the Labyrinth inside an old Realtor box, I placed welcome sheets as shown in italics so folks would have the opportunity to take part in this new prayer experience.

The Genesis Labyrinth Angel

Genesis Labyrinth

The Labyrinth mown into my front lawn is similar to the one in the Chartres Cathedral in France. You are welcome to walk this Labyrinth which I have named Genesis ... in joy, prayer, concern, love, and/or meditation. As you stand at the gate, take a deep breath ... let it out, leaving stress behind ... walk forward to the stone angel where you may choose a stone or object, if you wish, to carry as a symbol of whatever you need it to be. Carry this symbol, following the path, to the center. If you wish, you may leave it in the basket in the center of this sacred place in a physical act of turning your prayer over to God, or you may take it with you to remind you of the your prayer or of the peace you found here. Pause to meditate or pray if you wish. Then follow the path out of the Labyrinth with an open heart and gratitude for all the wonder of life. This place IS Sacred for it was created in Love and Compassion; and it is called Genesis to remind us of beginnings, journeys, turnings, and seeming endings that are really just new beginnings.

ABOUT THE LABYRINTH

A labyrinth is a pattern with a purpose, an ancient tool coming from Christian, Jewish, Native American, Egyptian, Asian, etc., churches and temples which speaks to a long forgotten part of us. Lying dormant for centuries, labyrinths are undergoing a revival of use and interest in many churches. They offer a chance to take "time out" from our busy lives, to leave schedules and stress behind. Walking a labyrinth is a gift we give to ourselves, leading to discovery, insight, peacefulness, happiness, connectedness, and well-being. The children walking Genesis Labyrinth call it a telephone to God.

The labyrinth represents our passage through time and experience. Its many turns reflect the journey of life, which involves change and transition, rites of passage, and cycles of nature. Different from a maze - which has dead ends and false passages - the labyrinth has a single path that leads unerringly to the center. It shows us that no time or effort is ever wasted - if we stay the course, every step, however circuitous, takes us closer to our goal.

Thinking is not required to walk a labyrinth. At the same time, one must remain alert to stay on the path. This combination of reduced mental activity and heightened awareness makes the labyrinth ideal for walking meditation or prayer. Some walk or dance the labyrinth just for the fun of it, or to express a particular intent or wish.

There is a strong connection between the labyrinth and earth energies, reestablishing a long-lost rapport with nature and with the feminine. The turns of the labyrinth are thought to balance the two hemispheres of the brain, resulting in physical and emotional healing. As reaching the center is assured, walking the labyrinth is more about the journey than the destination, about being rather than doing, integrating body and mind, psyche and spirit into one harmonious whole leading to a deep, inner experience. Thus, the labyrinth is really a tool, the physical entry point to the energy and truth that lie beyond the visible.

There is a reason why labyrinths have been passed down through the ages and used all over the world in myriad of cultural contexts. They are truly archetypes, based on the earth and the movement of the planets and the solar system. So are we, but we have forgotten that. Labyrinths awaken in us ancient memories, joining together that which is scattered, restoring our balance, and organizing our chaos, speaking to us through intuition and creative inspiration. Many Labyrinth walkers report "miracles" for the clarity of a balanced mind and spirit brings awareness that appears as answered prayer in that the walker becomes aware of the answers.

Labyrinths reduce our stress, reorder our priorities, and lead us to ourselves. We are Divine beings. The closer we get to our Self, the closer we get to God. Pierre Teillard de Chardin wrote of the "omega point," that point that we discover by going within, at which All That Is becomes revealed to us. Hence, walking a labyrinth is a sacred act, leading to the creation of labyrinths built into the floor or grounds of many of the world's great cathedrals and temples, as well as simple gathering places of prayer.

Some people took the Angel basin stones with them, and some put them back into the birdbath. But all who talked about this physical representation of their time of prayer here spoke of how much those objects meant to them, both to help them focus during their walking meditation and as a reminder and connection to the prayers they experienced.

Mostly, I didn't notice folks walking the Labyrinth. It's open to anyone to walk and is registered on a Labyrinth Finders website[5]. I've had folks call from as far away as New York to ask about walking it, but at the time of this incident I now share, no one had called about the Labyrinth for a couple of months.

My driveway is such a joy. That's an odd thing to say, but it's true. Being 175 feet long and about 15 to nearly 40 feet wide at the back, it is the best Garage Sale driveway I've ever seen. It is also so very handy for parking my motor home.

When I have a garage sale, I usually sleep in the motor home because folks come mighty early to sales around here, and they think nothing of taking the tarps off your tables before you're even out of your pajamas. I sleep in the motor home in my clothes so I can hear them coming and be up and about for those pre-dawn snoopers.

This particular pre-garage sale night, I was just lying down for sleep in the motor home. It must have been around midnight when I heard the sound of vehicles pulling into the driveway.

---

[5] http://wwll.veriditas.labyrinthsociety.org/ Type in my zip code 64052 to see a photo of my Genesis Labyrinth.

I sat up and peeked out the window. Two large vans were parking. The doors opened and about 15 or 16 young women got out. They circled up, bowed their heads, and prayed in silence. Then one at a time they entered the Labyrinth, walking slowly with hands lifted in receiving prayer. I watched as they walked, my heart gladdened that people were here and praying. It was magical and made tending the Labyrinth so worthwhile. Just as quietly, the girls circled up again after they had all exited the Labyrinth, prayed again, then climbed back into the vans and left.

I fell asleep, feeling so wonderful about the whole thing, grateful that I was blessed to witness their prayer and grateful that folks were coming to walk in prayer.

One day, three little boys rode up on their bikes. Curious, they asked what this thing in my yard was. They were about 9 or 10 years old, so my explanation was geared to their needs. I talked to them about prayer and how a path like this helped the brain to pray and to think better. They thought this was pretty cool, and asked a lot questions about what they could pray for. I shared with them about how answer to prayer often requires action, and always requires gratitude.

One boy said he wanted to pray for his Grandmother who was sick. I told him that such a prayer was wonderful but that there were things required of him as part of his prayer. We talked about the kinds of things he could do on his own without being asked. I suggested that when he visit her, that he try to do things for her and together we came up with several activities: bring her things, read to her, move quietly and slowly around her, rub her feet or her shoulders, share happy stories with her, ask her about her happy stories, or just play quietly at her feet while his parents visited with her.

Another boy wanted to know if it was okay to pray about his spelling test. We talked very seriously about this, again referring to his responsibility to study. I told him that walking the Labyrinth would help him to remember his words but that he still had to study. He nodded and I could see that these words gave him confidence that he could learn to spell better.

The third boy was worried about his dad. He'd lost his job and couldn't find another one. We brainstormed what actions he could take to help his dad. Prayer, of course, was at the top of the list, and then he came up with ideas to back up his prayer. "I'll keep my room cleaned up and pick up my toys so he doesn't get upset. I'll bring him the paper to read. I'll rub his shoulders and tell him I love him." The boy said.

The children were so excited to feel useful and helpful. I often saw them out there racing through the Labyrinth. They would ride their bikes full speed into the driveway, leap off them and run the Labyrinth. If they saw me, they would yell out whatever it was that was the subject of their prayer. "Math test tomorrow!" "Mom's mad." "I need a new bike!" Etc.

~~~~~~~~~~~~~~~~~~~~~~~~~~~~~~~~~~

A lady who lives around the corner often brings her small children at least once a week to walk the Labyrinth. She told me that she had read somewhere that Labyrinth walking was very good for the neurological development in children. Her children are old enough to come on their own now, and they enjoy running and playing in the Labyrinth.

During that first year of my retirement and my Labyrinth, my sewer backed up. Disgusting smell. One plumber broke his snake in the line. And I knew I was in big trouble financially.

They ran a video camera through my sewer line. Several bids later, I was resigned to the fact that the sewer repair would cost about $4,000 that I did not have. Tree roots had invaded my sewer lines and portions of the sewer pipe were cracked, broken or collapsed. My yard would have to be torn up for a new sewer line, and the hole would be at least 12 feet deep. The only good thing about it was that it was in the side and back yard and would not affect the Labyrinth.

Living off my savings because I was not old enough to qualify for my retirement for another year, I knew my savings had no room for a new sewer. I was living very frugally, knowing exactly how long my savings would last. On the Friday night after all the sewer bids had come in, I went out to walk the Labyrinth. I walked in gratitude for my ability to pay my bills and to pay for this sewer, even though I knew I didn't have the money. I walked with the thoughts about the lilies of the fields, "ask and ye shall receive," and every other quote I could remember from the Bible that applied. Then, I scheduled the repair.

On Monday, a check came in the mail for about $3,500. Totally unexpected. I was astonished. I had signed up for a class action suit several years previously, expecting to only get about $100 or so. My share turned out to be exactly what I needed to pay for the sewer once the city came to do part of the work. What a welcome miracle that was! Maybe the check would have come anyway, but I can't help thinking that the Lord – through my Labyrinth –had something to do with this entire experience. Combined with my savings, the city's share of the job, and decent weather keeping utilities low, it was exactly what I needed, not a penny more or a penny less.

When the tornado sirens would begin blaring or severe weather was predicted, I would run outside and walk the

Labyrinth in prayer that we would receive just enough rain or snow to nourish the plants and grass, and just enough wind to blow away any leaves I hadn't raked up. Often a ray of sunshine would bathe the Labyrinth while precipitation would begin outside my yard. The worst of the storms usually broke and split to go around us. My sister would get 6 inches of snow, ice, or flooding ten miles to the north, my school would get 6 inches ten miles to the east, and I'd get half of what they got. It was so consistently happening that friends, though mystified, were convinced.

During the years my mother lived in the Carriage House, my brother was starting a well repair business in Florida. Whenever things got slow and calls were not coming, my brother Rory would call my mother and ask her to walk the Labyrinth for him. She would always go right out, walk it, and pray for him. He always said that he'd then get a call within 24 hours.

~~~~~~

Rory began coming to visit each autumn to help me by repairing anything that needed fixing around my house. A Jack of all trades, he did this when his work in Florida was slow, and he needed to get away for awhile. These trips began after he learned the trouble I was having with handy-men who seemed to think it was okay to lie, over-charge, and cheat me just because I was a woman alone.

Rory was fascinated by the Labyrinth, loved hearing the latest stories about Labyrinth walkers, and was overjoyed about what a difference it made for him with his water-well-repair business. He also loves to tell the story of how his gall-bladder was full of stones but an operation could not be done because his thyroid cancer had left him too fragile to tolerate another surgery so soon.

When Rory came to visit that first year, he spent a great of time in the Labyrinth, praying for healing. One day, he was surprised and grateful to find he had easily passed all the gall stones in one long visit to the bathroom. He's not had any trouble with his gall bladder since then.

One year, Rory brought a friend from Florida whom he had known for a long time. Betty had been in a very bad car accident. The doctors wanted to cage her spine because the fractures in her back were so bad that they could not be repaired. She had been in a great deal of pain for a couple of years and could barely walk. Bent over nearly 30 degrees, she just shuffled along. Rory had brought her along on this trip because she was so depressed; he was deeply worried about her.

Betty's appetite was very poor. She slept a lot, was in constant pain, and was miserable. I was very puzzled about why he would bring her when she was so obviously ill. All she did was sleep, read, and drink tea the first few days. But Rory had spent much of the drive from Florida telling Betty stories about the Labyrinth.

Finally I told Rory he needed to get her up, dressed, and brought downstairs. I was worried because she was not eating, and was only drinking tea. When she came downstairs, weak and bent over, I tried to get her to eat some soup I'd made but she wouldn't. I pulled Rory out the back door to talk to him about her, asking what we should do. I told him that she would die if she didn't eat. The woman was gray, and she even smelled bad. We talked for a while about our options, both of us very worried. I told Rory in no uncertain terms that we had to do something.

When we went back inside, I thought Betty must have gone back upstairs because she was not at the kitchen table. Rory ran up to check on her but came back down and went into the living room to see if she was there. Then he softly called my name. When I went into the living room, I saw he was standing at the front door. "Look," he said. "She's walking the Labyrinth."

We stood and watched as she very slowly began inching through the Labyrinth. Her gait was incredibly slow and uneven, and we were concerned she might trip and fall. Suddenly Rory grabbed my arm, and excitedly whispered, "She's straightening up. Do you see?" With bated breath, we watched Betty very slowly begin to walk more and more upright. She still walked very slowly but it seemed as though she wasn't dragging her feet as much, and gradually her head was lifting up.

Rory went outside to wait for her as she made her way out of the Labyrinth. Neither of us said anything about her stance ... we just watched her as her posture gradually straightened. I think perhaps we didn't quite believe what we were seeing and were afraid to say anything, fearful we might jinx it. Betty came into the kitchen and went to the refrigerator to get her tea. She set her tea on the countertop, stopped and stood there for a second staring straight ahead ... and suddenly ... when the awareness of her posture hit her ... she screamed. "Oh my God, I'm standing up straight. Oh, my God. Oh my God."

After going to a mirror to look at herself standing up straight, Betty discovered she was hungry ... for the first time in months, she was hungry and was finally ready to eat something. My friend John had cooked up a huge batch of fresh bass, and Betty stood there at the kitchen counter, and ate just about the whole plateful. She never walked with her back bent again. She was overjoyed. Her family was astonished when she returned to Florida able to move freely, happily, and with her natural vibrancy returned.

The healing remained and she was able to get on with her life. Rory saw her again years later, and she was still walking perfectly.

Prayers for General Needs

Divine love fills the universe, guiding and protecting me. I thank God for the light, love and power active in my life. I am filled with joy and happiness and I gratefully accept God's bountiful goodness, healing, and blessings.

I flow through the changes before me, sustained by God's unconditional love and grace. I accept all the right and perfect order God has for me. I give thanks for the new, dynamic, positive choices available to me. Through the Christ within, I choose wisely for my best and highest good. The choices I make bring forth the changes I need for my spiritual and emotional growth

Prayers for Healing

God is love, and I am beloved. God is light, and I am guided to my highest good. God is health, and I am whole in every way. God is unlimited supply, and my life is prospered. My needs are met, and I rejoice in the bounty of blessings pouring forth into my life.

Part Two

Traveling

EIGHT

Being Called

The next part of this story comprises about six months from September of 2005 through February of 2006. However it also puts together bits and pieces of nearly 33 years of this-and-that odd synchronicities, puzzling moments, and questions. For the sake of the story, I think it is best to begin in September of 2005 at the beginning of the end, or is it the end of the beginning?

A huge part of what I have been dealing with since my retirement is the big question concerning finding the purpose of my life. Consistently the unease, the angst, the wonder of what I am supposed to be doing has followed me around, dogging my steps like a rock in my shoe or a puppy nipping at the hem of my jeans. Once in a while, that question overwhelmed daily life and I was forced to confront it. Usually it occurred when John and I were being faced with the reality of how different we were and how difficult our love for one another had become through those differences. We'd come through the Presidential election year at each other's throats, and the lingering effects of that ongoing argument hovered over our heads and hearts.

John was a Right-Wing-Conservative-Republican, Gun-Toting-Hunter-Fisherman and Fundamentalist-Southern-Baptist, all of which are capitalized because each was a deep passion for him. I am a student of religions, attending

Unitarian and later Unity churches, after being raised Catholic, getting excommunicated after my divorce in 1978, and exploring Methodist, Assembly of God, Lutheran, Jewish, Hindu, Rosicrucian, etc. etc. etc. I am also an intellectual Liberal Democrat, along with being an artist, poet, storyteller, teacher, home remodeler, and writer. We were very different.

One day in early October of '05, I walked the Labyrinth in frustration and yearning to know what I needed to be doing. I was so at the end of my rope that I didn't care what the answer was, I just wanted to know. I've found this *not caring, not attaching expectation parameters to my prayer attitude* to be one of the most important components of answered prayer.

Experience was teaching me one step at a time that the best answers come from a place where I put no stipulations or boundaries on the answers, as if God needed to be free to give me what was the best for me without my mind interfering. It was truly about being open to the best and not closed by my own fears or expectations.

Finishing my Labyrinth walk and angst-filled prayer that September day, still not feeling much relief and seeking something to counter the agitation, I looked around for something to do. The desire to thwart the mental turmoil with action led me up to the third floor where I began cleaning out an old trunk, telling myself that I was honoring my efforts to simplify my life. Too much stuff! Too much restlessness. Too much agitation.

In the bottom of the trunk was a lithograph that a dear artist friend, Randy Read, had created of a waterfall which was inspired by a photo from my "Magic of Findhorn" book. I sat and just looked at that lithograph, recalling my interest in Findhorn Garden back in the early seventies, wondering where my "Magic of Findhorn" book was, and also wondering if Findhorn Garden was still there in Scotland. Setting the lithograph aside, I continued cleaning out the trunk as I allowed my thoughts to drift elsewhere, away from Scotland and into unremembered avenues.

Later that afternoon, I went downstairs and checked my e-mail. With the opposing ideological issues confronting John and me, we were separated. I had signed up for eHarmony, hoping to meet someone closer to my own pathway, my own interests, and especially my own spirituality. This particular afternoon, eHarmony had sent a new name to me, so I pulled up his profile and began reading.

Imagine my surprise when the man referred to me had written that the most influential folks in his life were Eileen and Peter Caddy, the co-founders of Findhorn Garden.

Twice in one day, the two words "Findhorn Garden" had appeared in my life ... two words that had not been seen, heard or spoken by me for decades. I'd first learned of Findhorn back in the late '60s and early 70s, but my life had led me in different directions. The appearance of these two words was interesting and surprising but didn't register on my mind enough to make me pay attention. It wasn't until that evening when I took my weekly visit to the library, that I finally woke up and took notice.

The magic of three seemed to be in action.[6] [*Even Aristotle said that people tend to remember things that happen in threes.*] And that night as I stood looking at books in the fiction section of the library, the third event arrived in the form of a quiet voice. I was perusing books back in the stacks, and I heard someone

[6]*For more information on the magic of three, see: https://en.wikipedia.org/wiki/Rule_of_three_(writing)*

in the next aisle over utter the words: "Findhorn Garden." I jumped - literally jumped - then scooted around the end of the aisle to see who had spoken. NO ONE was there. This time I paid attention.

The minute I got home, finally aware that a message was being offered with these synchronistic events, I went to my computer and typed "Findhorn Garden" into Google. There I found their website, and I began to read. The thing that stood out on that page on that day was the article titled "Essence of the Arts" program.

I clicked on it, and with mounting excitement read about this program or 'programme' as it is spelled in Scotland. Something inside of me leapt with joy, and I knew - I KNEW - without a doubt that I *must* do this. I called my mother who was living in my Carriage House at that time to come over right away to read something. I told her about the three times I'd heard 'Findhorn Garden' that day, and that I'd found something on the internet that I HAD TO DO. She came, and after reading the article about the Essence of the Arts programme, turned to me and said with the full force of a mother's authority "You have to do this!"[7]

I didn't have the money. After converting pounds into dollars and checking airline fares, I found that it would cost more than $7,000. Whoa! But I knew I had to do it. So I began researching where to get the money.

The next day, I went to my bank, thinking I would take out a Line of Credit, perhaps a second mortgage, or a loan of some kind to pay for this. When I explained to my banker what I wanted to do, he became excited about this trip for me. He lowered his voice and conspiratorially recommended that I

[7] ***See*** *www.Findhorn.org*

take out a 0% interest credit card from the bank and charge everything on it .... Then if I couldn't pay it back in time, to take out another and transfer the balance. His quiet voice hid the fact that he was recommending something that would help me very much but not necessarily benefit the bank. So that's what I did.

From the bank, I went to Walgreen's, had a passport picture taken, and with photo in hand, I headed to the Post Office to apply for a passport. I had less than a month to get all my ducks in a row for this trip.

I did it! A whirlwind is the best word for the next three weeks. People went out of their way to help. Because my stepdad adopted us in New Jersey after my father's suicide, the passport authority said they could not accept an adoption birth certificate, and that I must get an original. Fearing that the closing of adoption records would affect this, I nervously called the little town where I was born and was referred to the county office.

When I told the clerk in the county office of Roseau, Minnesota, who handled all county business including birth records about the trip, she also became excited for me. She made a special effort to find a copy of my original birth certificate and send it. She took it to the Post Office on her lunch break, paid for it out of her own pocket to overnight it to me, sure I would reimburse her right away (which, of course, I did).

At that time (2005), passports from Kansas City were processed in New Orleans, however, because of Hurricane Katrina, New Orleans was shut down. Kansas City area applications were farmed out to other cities, and they couldn't tell me where it would go. So I got on the phone and began calling Passport Offices across the country.

After several episodes of just getting recordings, finally a real person in the New Hampshire office answered the phone. Once again, a complete stranger became so enthusiastic and excited about my trip, she instructed me to send my application materials directly to her and to overnight them. She called me when she got them, and did them while on the phone with me. Then once again, my papers were sent in over-night mail to me by a kind caring person who was willing to slip out of the office on her break and run them to the Post Office. This time, I'd enclosed a money order made out to her for the postage.

Everything was completed, from arrangements for my automatic bill payments to scheduling folks to keep an eye on my 83-year-old-mother while I was gone. I left for Scotland on October 26th and did not arrive home again until the first week of February.

Findhorn Garden - How do I describe that experience? So much happened, so many epiphanies, so much joy and so many traumas. Where do I begin?

Prayers for Prosperity

I stand firm in faith that my needs are already fulfilled, and I look past the appearance of lack and limitation to the truth that God is my unlimited supply. My health, happiness and prosperity are assured. When there seems to be no way, God opens a way – God is in the midst of this experience. God is the True Source of my income. I am lovingly blessed with abundance, success, and prosperity.

Prayers for Travel

Wherever you are, wherever you go, you are under Divine Protection. God is everywhere present, providing faith, courage, and strength for you. You are always protected.

Prayers for Inner Peace

You are one with the infinite life of God that supports you in every moment. You release all worry and anxiety and discover a new sense of balance. You are at peace as you perform your tasks easily and with grace. Your mind and heart are filled with peace.

NINE

First Week at Findhorn

After nearly eighteen hours on two different planes, a couple hours on a bus, and finally a half mile walk in the dark along Findhorn Bay to a seaside Bed & Breakfast Cottage, I was welcomed by a large friendly family anxious to serve me some delicious hot soup and freshly made bread. I fell into bed for a good night's sleep and was awakened deliciously by the scent of coffee brewing and bread baking.

Joining the family for breakfast was a delight. They offered to take my luggage to Cluny Hotel, and gave me directions on walking to Findhorn Park from the Cottage, where I was to check-in and later catch the shuttle to the Hotel.

Before beginning any programmes at Findhorn, visitors are usually asked to first do "Experience Week" which is led by long-time residents at Cluny Hotel in Forres, only a few kilometers from Findhorn Park (the Findhorn Gardens is now known officially as Findhorn Park). These leaders take turns hosting groups of visitors as they learn the protocols to living in this unique community, learning the history, and visiting the places where that history took place.

We learned how prayer begins and ends <u>every</u> activity. We explored sacred woodland meadows, copses, rivers, paths, and rooms both inside various buildings and inside hillsides.

We learned to listen to the Grandfather trees, ancient magnificent fellows standing guard in this historic land. I loved it and felt so spiritually alive and connected through these prayers, meditations, and walks through this magical land.

We were invited and encouraged to become an integral part of the community ... spending half of each day in group activities, and half in giving/tithing our labor to the community.

Findhorn is run by the Findhorn Foundation with some activities held at Cluny Hotel and many others at both Findhorn Park and adjoining Cullerne Gardens. My Experience Week days usually went something like this:

> 7:30 a.m. Breakfast in Cluny Dining Room, then shuttled to Findhorn Garden's "The Park"
> 8:30 a.m. Meditation in the Main Sanctuary
> 9:00 a.m. Walking to the gardens to do my
> **Tithing labor:** *(Everyone, resident and visitors alike, all tithe their time and labor to some form of work at Findhorn)*

On the second day of Experience Week, we were introduced to how Findhorn does things. Focalizers from various departments visited our group for a few minutes on the first day to let us know how many helpers they needed for the week, telling us that in order to truly experience Findhorn, we would become part of the community through helping in all areas.

We were told to trust our highest selves in choosing which department to join: kitchen, gardens, house-keeping, maintenance, laundry, etc. As they described the various jobs, my first thought was that I wanted to work in the kitchen because I wanted to learn how to prepare the amazing vegan food we had enjoyed at our first day's meals. I did not want the gardens because I have a bad back and figured I couldn't do that kind of work. Then we were told to close our eyes as our focalizers prayed for guidance for each of us to choose the job in which our highest selves knew was where we belonged.

I committed to following my highest self's guidance. With closed eyes, we were told to raise our hands when the right job was named. We were also told that the number of helpers requested was consistently achieved during this closed eyes experience. As I waited for the kitchen job to be named while also reinforcing my desire to follow Spirit, imagine my surprise and chagrin when my hand shot up when the gardens were named.

Even though it was the one job my logical mind did not want, it turned out to be the perfect job for me. The man I ended up working alongside for that week was a young fellow with AIDS from Belgium who was studying at Findhorn with the goal of creating a place like Findhorn for AIDS patients back home. We talked. And we talked and talked and talked. And one for the other, we each facilitated an epiphany of sorts. We came together that week for a very definite purpose and were both so very grateful.

The work was easy for me … just gently brushing dried dirt from bulbs before storing them for the winter … work which allowed for lots of quiet sharing and talking, and no strain on my back at all.

Findhorn Garden was famous for 40-pound cabbages. The basis of the garden was, and still is, working in harmony and co-creation with nature. Working at Cullerne Gardens during Experience Week was magical.

10:30 a.m. Tea with jam and warm freshly baked bread ... scrumptious ... then, back to work, which was a complete joy to perform.

Mid-morning tea with jam and bread

Garden Shed at Cullerne Gardens

Noon: Return to Cluny Hotel for lunch and afternoon sessions.

1 to 5 p.m. Afternoon session with a break halfway through for hot bread, jam, and tea. Sometimes we went on field trips, sometimes we listened to speakers share their Findhorn experiences, knowledge, philosophy, history, and inner workings.

These discussions were food for my soul. They marked the first time where my unusual life experiences were okay, the first time my psychic nature was not seen as 'evil', and the first time I wasn't afraid to share those experiences and abilities.

In the evenings, we all had dinner together in the dining room. We often gathered later for long walks, singing, reading, or just visiting.

November roses blooming on Cluny Hotel where Experience Week is held.

My Grandfather Tree

Riverside Walking Meditation trail.

"Prayer for Working in the Gardens"

"Bless the work of our hands, and let it be a blessing for all those who also work here in the gardens. Bless these plants which are going to feed and nourish our bodies and the bodies of all who eat here. Bless our fellowship as we work together in harmony, in peace, and in love for what we do here and for one another. Bless us, for we are honored to do this work, we are blessed to be able to give, and blessed to be able to receive. Bless the divas of these gardens and of these plants, who work silently and invisibly with us to nurture these plants. We are grateful for this time together with each other and the divas, and grateful for the opportunity to be channels of blessings for all who benefit from the work of our hands."

TEN

Programme Friends?
{Or Roses with Thorns}

Having completed Experience Week at Cluny Hotel in Forres[8], I moved to Findhorn Park Guest Lodge to begin my next programme, Essence of the Arts in Community.

Findhorn Park Guest Lodge

The members of my Essence of the Arts in Community group were our focalizers, Georgette from Brazil and Desie from

---

[8] *https://www.findhorn.org/aboutus/community/cluny/*

Sweden. Antonio, from Portugal; Zoe (a dancer) and Lesley (a nurse) from England; Martine, (age 17) from Norway; Camilla, from Sweden; James, from the USA; Almut, (an MD) from Germany; Sally (an artist) and her boyfriend Nigel from England; V. and Olivia (a dancer) from Belgium: Jan and Robyn, (both retirees) from Australia.

Jan became my closest friend as we took part in another Findhorn tradition. We became co-listening partners. We walked together each evening after dinner for at least 30 minutes. Everyone at Findhorn is encouraged to form a co-listener partnership. Co-listeners listen to each other without comment. They take turns talking things out without judgment, without advice, without any reaction except compassionate listening. It's a practice which convinced me that one person could listen another into finding their own answers.

Robyn had signed up to come to Findhorn after learning that Jan, who was an acquaintance in Australia, was coming for this three month experience. Jan was not terribly happy about Robyn intruding on her trip. She had decided to just grin and bear it but also to stand her ground about making sure this trip was hers alone.

{Jan and I had shared a room at Cluny Hotel during the first week in Scotland while we took part in Experience Week so we had a week to form a friendship before Robyn arrived.}

Robyn wanted to be Jan's co-listening partner, and she was very upset when Jan decided to be my partner. Weeks went by, and because I am a bit of a loner anyway, I didn't really notice anything amiss until one Friday during our weekly group gathering when we each had an opportunity to share how things were going. It was the one time each week when each group member spoke to the entire group. We were free to speak about anything we wished and the group listened.

That Friday something happened completely unexpectedly. Robyn got up to share, and came and stood in front of me. She said. "I hate you. I hate you. I cannot stand to be around you. I tried to get my lodging changed so I wouldn't have to live in the same building as you. I tried to get my money back so I could go home, but they would not give it to me. I hate you. I cannot stand your face. I cannot stand looking at you; I cannot stand being around you. I hate you." Then she sat down.

I was shocked. More than shocked. I was reeling. There had been no problems between Robyn and me so I didn't know what she was talking about. I took a couple of deep breaths, knowing that I had done nothing to deserve this treatment. No one in the group said a word about this, and the next person simply stood up to share their own things. When it was my turn, I slowly rose and walked over to stand in front of Robyn.

"I do not know why you hate me Robyn, but I do not hate you." I said quietly. "I believe that whatever you feel is wrong is something that we can work out."

Immediately Robyn screamed at me, "This is one of the things I cannot stand about you. Everything is 'WE' with you. You don't own anything. You have no right to include me in your 'WE'. The sneer in her voice was like knives in my heart.

At that point, several people broke in to say "She said 'I believe' It is her belief. She is saying she believes you can work it out. There is nothing wrong with what she said."

I was deeply confused. I could not figure out why she was attacking me. I didn't understand what she was objecting to in my speech. I did not understand what I'd done wrong, as I used "we" a lot with my young students to help them learn that all people experience many of the same emotions and/or reactions to events. It's a word usage designed to take the sting out of painful or embarrassing moments in their lives.

No one spoke to me about what Robyn had said. No one comforted me except Jan, my co-listener, who when I asked, spoke of her experience that Robyn had a tendency to rock the boat in Australia, hence was one of the reasons she had not wanted her to come on this trip.

I was devastated, not only because of what Robyn had said. Robyn appeared to be close friends with all the others in the group - but because I felt I had no support except Jan, which was perhaps my own fault, as I had allowed my shyness to keep me fairly quiet in group.

I spent the next few days walking ... alone. I took daily walks across the dunes to the sea, along the shore to Findhorn Village, then back to The Park along the Moray Firth and Findhorn Bay. I walked in the mist, in the rain, in the cold ... too stunned to even cry, head down, and trying to breathe. Gradually I rejoined the group, but I stayed quiet and withdrawn.

Prayers for Inner Peace

Even in the midst of circumstances that you may not understand, you affirm that God's love and peace are strengthening you, and preparing the way for your inner peace and comfort. You are one with the infinite life of God that supports you in every moment. You release all worry and anxiety and discover a new sense of balance. You are at peace as you perform your tasks easily and with grace. Your mind and heart are filled with peace.

Prayer for Difficult Circumstances

I behold the Christ in others, however challenging the circumstances. Everything and everyone is my teacher, and I open myself to the divine lesson I am to learn. If I am upset or disturbed, I pray: "Help me see this differently, God." I patiently await divine guidance on what to say and do. I trust the still, small voice within me to guide me in right ways to express myself honestly and lovingly, and to listen with an open heart. All is made clear and my relationships come into perfect order and alignment. Thank you, God, for the wisdom that leads to compassion and understanding.

Eleven

Findhorn Sanctuary

The first clue of why I was called to Findhorn Garden, Scotland happened in the middle of the night a few weeks after arriving, when I woke suddenly and couldn't go back to sleep. Findhorn is different than American communities. There are no streetlights; starlight is the order of the night. Everyone walks wherever they go. I rose, dressed, and decided to walk over to the Sanctuary.

The Sanctuary at Findhorn

It was open as it always is, this place of constant prayer and meditation. For more than 40 years, people have come from all over the world to pray there. At 3 in the morning, I had the Sanctuary to myself. I sat down and began to meditate.

I knew that Eileen Caddy had spent every night of her life at Findhorn in prayer and meditation, writing down the words of wisdom she heard from God.

As I sat there in silence, feeling I wasn't good enough to hear like Eileen did, still I listened, just in case.

I was comfortable, sitting there in this lovely place where I'd lit the candles on the low table in the center of the room. Soft light, soft chair, soft breeze outside brushing branches gently against the walls. I heard the door open, and I felt the cool breeze wash over me. Someone walked into the room, and I was not afraid. I felt safe and kept my eyes closed.

The unseen person walked closer, and I sensed he was watching me, but I kept my eyes closed, trying to be nonchalant and too cool to be affected. However, he - and somehow I knew it was a "he" - came and sat down in the chair right beside me to my left. Now that was creepy. There were at least 40 gold chairs to choose from, and plenty of room on the carpeted floor also, so sitting right next to me felt threatening.

Now I was unnerved, so I opened my eyes a tiny bit and peeked to my left. NO ONE was there. Taking a deep breath, I closed my eyes again and listened. Nothing. I peeked again. Still no one was there. I reminded myself that Eileen Caddy had done this for 45 years, so finally I found the courage to ask, "Who is there?"

A chuckle accompanied the answer I heard spoken. "Saint Germain". I was startled and chagrined, and now I was definitely frightened. I called on Jesus to come because "Saint Germain" was a name that had haunted me since the early 70's and I didn't know what to do with it.

And lo and behold, Jesus came. I sensed Him sitting down beside me on my right. I could see him in my mind's eye, and I felt His peace soothing me as I remembered all the times this Saint Germain fellow had intruded upon my life. I felt safe with Jesus there, who also spoke, saying, "It's okay, he is my friend".

{Note: all of the events leading to this moment in the Sanctuary are detailed in Chapter Twelve}

Wondering if I was losing my mind and drawing on the bit of anger and frustration over this Saint Germain thing, I said strongly and maybe even aloud. "I want to see you with my physical eyes. Show yourself to me!" I commanded, directing my words to Saint Germain.

I felt Saint Germain answer with a smile. "You will see me later today," He said. With that, they both faded from my mind's eye. I sat for awhile longer, and then knew it was time to go back to my room and go to bed.

The next morning, we were informed at breakfast that our usual Friday gathering would not be in the Park Building's lecture room but would be held in the Sanctuary in the Park Building. Most of us, me included, had no idea there was a Sanctuary in the Park Building. This usual Friday meeting was our time to share whatever we wanted to share about whatever! Usually folks in my group talked about insights or questions they were dealing with. Sometimes poetry or writings were shared. It was a special time for us each week to check in with the group about where we were inside of ourselves.

I walked with my co-listening partner, Jan, over to the Park Building, talking about this and that … but not ready to share my 'mid-night' experience with anyone yet. I feared they would think I was truly nuts.

When Jan and I reached the Park Building, someone led the way to the door into the Sanctuary, a door I had just not noticed even though I was in that building for part of every day. As it turned out, I was the first to enter the Sanctuary. It was a Lavender room with a fireplace and a few aqua-colored comfortable chairs. Being the second oldest in the group, I went to claim one of those chairs, as the condition of my creaky knees had ordained in our group: if there was chair, I got it. I sat down and looked around.

The Park Building Sanctuary was a lovely, peaceful room, the colors so sweet and calmly refreshing. The aqua-colored chairs and accessories set off the lavender walls and carpet in a way that touched my senses. On the wall opposite me was a painting of a man. He was very pale, very white. I'm not sure whether the artist had done the painting so whitely on purpose or if it had faded over the years. I could tell the painting was very old. I sat looking at it while the others came in and made themselves comfortable.

As Georgette, our focalizer (group leaders at Findhorn are called focalizers) came through the door, I rather flippantly asked her, "Who is the ghost on the wall?" referring to the whiteness of his countenance.

Smiling brightly, Georgette replied, "That's Saint Germain."

Saint Germaine's Sanctuary in the Park Building

I screamed, and fell off my chair. I began to cry. I was furious, and I didn't know why. I was scared and angry and completely out of control for a few minutes. Everyone was shocked. So was I.

When I finally calmed down, I was able to tell everyone how it seemed Saint Germain had followed me all my life. I told them some of the stories and the puzzlement. "Why is he here?" I asked Georgette.

"The Patron Saint of Findhorn is Saint Germain," She replied.

I felt tricked ... like it was a huge practical joke that had brought me here. I was inexplicably angry, so terribly angry.

Georgette suggested that I go into the library next door and check out some books about the role of Saint Germain in the formation of Findhorn Garden. She also suggested that I talk to Craig, one of our pottery focalizers, who had been at Findhorn since the beginning and was personally acquainted with Saint Germain.

Georgette

Craig

My mind was reeling. Like he had promised, I saw Saint Germain that day. Yes, it was in a portrait, an antique portrait, but still I saw his face.

At lunch, I made arrangements to meet with Craig the next day. Then I went to the library and found the books I needed to read. It would take me a couple of weeks to get through the books. They were almost more than I could take. Some of what I read went against the grain of my sense of right and wrong. Whether it was my sense that was wrong or what I read as being right or wrong is still to be determined in my mind.

My meeting with Craig helped more than anything. He listened to my stories of the encounters with the idea of Saint Germain. He laughed when I described how angry I was at feeling tricked into coming to Findhorn. He told me that many people came to Findhorn with claims of being connected to Saint Germain, sharing how he could always tell who was telling the truth, and who was fantasizing or engaging in wishful thinking. Because he and Peter Caddy had so much experience with Saint Germain, they knew him like one friend knows another. Craig said that what I described was exactly how Saint Germain would handle it.

"He loves a good practical joke," Craig said. "The way you got here is exactly something he would do, so I know that the connection between you and Saint Germain is real and important, and everything will be okay."

Craig went on to advise me to stay open, stay grounded, respect my doubts, work with them, but to not let fear hold me in bondage. He also told me that the book I'd gotten from Chicago (explained in Chapter 12) was one of those written by someone who wasn't truly in touch with Saint Germain, but wished they were. "Answers would come and I was on the right path" were the promises I took away from our talk.

Throughout my stay at Findhorn, Saint Germain often came to me in the Sanctuary during my meditations. I was afraid of him, so each time, I called on Jesus to be with me. It was great. Jesus would come and sit down beside me, and I felt safe. I just didn't know what to make of this entity named Saint Germain, even though he and Jesus seemed to be friends.

I just didn't know what to believe, and I didn't trust. I was holding him at arm's length and in a way, even to this day, I am holding him at arm's length.

Prayers for Protection

When you feel threatened, you remind yourself that the presence and power of God is all there is. Nothing can stand against God. There is no other power. You focus on God, and know that God is mightier than any circumstance. You are always divinely protected.

The Prayer of Protection
Written by James Dillet Freeman

The Light of God surrounds you.
The Love of God enfolds you.
The power of God protects you.
The Presence of God watches over you.

The Mind of God guides you.
The Life of God flows through you.
The Laws of God direct you.
The Peace of God abides within you.

The Joy of God uplifts you.
The Strength of God renews you.
The Beauty of God inspires you.
Wherever you are, God is!
And all is well. Amen.[9]

---

[9] *https://www.unitychurch.org/prayer-protection*

TWELVE

Saint Germain

My history with Saint Germain occurred over many years, with seemingly unrelated events which came together at Findhorn, and are detailed here, in order of occurrence.

The early '70s:
During the early days of my marriage, my husband and I were living in a little house at Lake Lotawana, MO.

One night I awoke with a creative itch ... a very strong desire to draw or paint.

Getting up and looking around, I saw the wooden shelf we used for our telephone. I took it off the wall, pulled out my oil pastels and did a picture on it of a monk – with no idea who he might be.

The early '80s: Divorced in 1978 and on my own, a time came when I was ill. Very ill, after a table fell on me at work causing hidden damage. My niece Glory had come to help take care of me for a few months. She was sleeping in bed with me so she could be close if I needed help.

One night, we had been talking about soul mates as we lay there together. I had been wondering if my boy-friend, Russ, was my soul mate. We fell asleep with this conversation on our minds.

In the night, she was awakened because I was talking in my sleep. The words coming from me were in a deep masculine sounding voice which held an authority that gave Glory the confidence to ask a question while at the same time was deeply puzzling to her, "Is Russ Aunt JanMarie's soul mate?" She asked.

"No." was the answer. "He was a French Viscount."

"Who is Aunt JanMarie's soul mate?" Glory asked.

And the strange voice coming from my mouth said, "Saint Germain." Glory then asked, "Who are you?"

The voice answered, "Brahman."

This was pre-internet days, so our sources of information were limited to the library. We could not find any information about this Saint Germain or Brahman. Even my college pastor Monsignor Feidler could find no information on him.

The late '80s: One evening, I was creating a backdrop for the Christmas Musical I had written and was directing for my 2nd graders at school. It was a 15-by-4.5 foot mural depicting a mountain in a starry winter's night. I had stayed late after school, and other than a night custodian, I was the only one in the building.

The picture, done with chalk pastels on lavender paper was going very rapidly, and to my astonishment was turning out quite lovely. The mountain I drew was completely from my imagination, and my hands flew over the paper as though in the control of something magical.

The picture was a huge success, and I received many compliments about it, so much so that I took photos of it, one of which is reproduced here:

Because bulletin board paper fades after a while, it is difficult to see how lovely it really was in this photo taken later

Mid '90s: For several summers in a row beginning in 1993, I had been going out to Anacortes, Washington in order to reconnect with my birth father's family and to explore the town of Anacortes where I had lived until my dad's death in 1957.

On the first trip out there, my cousin Pam had driven up from Portland to meet me. As part of our getting to know each other, I showed her my little portfolio of my artwork. When she saw the photo of the mountain drawing, she exclaimed. "Oh, you've been to Mt. Shasta!"

"No" I answered. "This was drawn from my imagination, one of those spontaneously fast teacher-in-a-hurry-with-too-much-to-do moments. I don't know anything about a Mt. Shasta. Where is it?"

Pam laughed and said. "We were just there. I have the photos here in my purse." And she pulled them out and began leafing through them.

"Look." She said as she handed me a photo which was taken from the same view I had unknowingly drawn a few years previously. I was astonished, puzzled, chagrined and quite unable to make sense of it.

In 1994, on another summer trip to Anacortes, I made friends with an art gallery owner named Charlotte Pettigrew. When she asked to see my portfolio, I shyly handed it over. I wasn't to the point of considering myself an artist yet. Most of my compliments came from 7 year olds so I assumed their comments were so tinged with their love for me that I couldn't really count appreciation of talent in there. As Charlotte was going through the photos of my artwork, she came upon the monk I had drawn so many years before.

"Oh, my God," she exclaimed. "It's Saint Germain!" This was the first time, I had heard those words since the sleep talking experience with Glory.

"Who is Saint Germain?" I asked with wonder and puzzlement.

Charlotte told me that she was friends with the wife of Burl Ives (the famous mid-century actor and ballad singer) who had a home there in Anacortes. She said that Mrs. Ives had a Sanctuary dedicated to Saint Germain in her home.

After I told Charlotte the circumstances of the drawing of the monk and the incident of the sleep talking, she said. "Mrs. Ives will want to see this and to hear this story" and she went to her phone to call the lady. Unfortunately, as Mrs. Ives housekeeper informed us, the couple was in California visiting family and would not return until after I was scheduled to go home.

Charlotte encouraged me to bring the actual oil pastel drawing with me the next time I came to Anacortes, and she promised she would take me to meet Mrs. Ives.

However, the following summer of 1995, the news was that Mr. Ives had passed away, and Mrs. Ives had gone to California to live, so I never met her nor did I find out anything about Saint Germain. However, Charlotte added to the mystery when she commented that answers about Saint Germain might be found at Mt. Shasta.

Late '90s. I had met this interesting and quite talented psychic woman (Linda) from St. Louis through a friend who knew she wanted to rent a room for a few days. We had made arrangements for her to come to stay at my house every few months to hold readings for folks in the Kansas City area.

One evening, Linda had gone out with some friends, and called to ask if she could bring them back to the house after dinner to visit with me. I agreed.

One of the ladies was a healer, and when she met me, she asked if I would allow her to do a healing on me. I assented immediately ... healings were always welcome. Toward the end of her session with me, she placed her hands on my head. She said, "Something or someone is telling me that Saint Germain is looking for you."

I sat right up. "What is Saint Germain? Who is Saint Germain?" I asked her. I told her of the incidents with my niece, the drawing of the monk, Mt. Shasta, and the Mrs. Ives thing. She gave me a phone number to call. The woman I called was in Chicago. She offered to send a book to me about Saint Germain.

The book arrived the next week, I read it and with disgust, sent it back to her. I thought it was crap. I knew it was crap. This Saint Germain stuff made no sense to me, and frankly, I really didn't want to have anything to do with the character I read about in that book. There seemed to be way too much emphasis on getting rich, on turning metals into gold, and other ideas with which I did not agree.

The Fall of 2000: I had a dinner engagement with an interesting fellow I had met at an Interfaith Conference in Kansas City. His name was Ahmed El-Sherif. He was the leader of the Muslim community at that time.

Over dinner at the Courthouse Exchange on Independence Square, he suddenly exclaimed, "I think you should go to my favorite place in the entire world. It is a sacred mountain here in the United States. I go there whenever I can. There is something there that is so special." His eyes misted as his mind took him to those memories of his visits. "And I feel strongly that you must go there," he said.

I raised my eyebrows, silently asking "why?" and "where?"

In answer, he took my hands, looked deeply into my eyes and said, "You must go to Mt. Shasta!" I remembered and finally registered at that moment that I had seen the words "Mt. Shasta" mentioned in the book sent to me about St. Germaine. My Muslim friend replied to my puzzlement about this. He told me Mt. Shasta was considered the home of Saint Germain.

Inside my mind, I rolled my eyes, and if truth be told, experienced a twinge of fear combined with a hint of annoyance.

Prayers for Guidance

God is my inner source of inspiration. God's loving guidance is always with me. Through prayer, I am guided to a greater understanding of all that is before me. I am calm and centered. I have a God-given ability to think clearly, to concentrate fully, and to express myself perfectly. I look to the Christ spirit for wisdom and direction. My way is clear and the Christ Light inspires me to take right action.

THIRTEEN

Essence of the Arts

Findhorn is blessed to be inhabited by the most amazing and diverse variety of individuals. This community of international artists, musicians, healers, and spiritual seekers of all kinds come from all over the world. I went to Findhorn for the art and for the spiritual connections I so deeply desired. Findhorn had everything I needed: opportunity, experience, music, creative writing, dance, movement, sculpture, drama, spiritual connections and experiences with those of similar mindfulness.

Each of the arts is its own story. I'll begin with the day when artist's chalk, a large piece of black paper, meditation, and openness permitted an uncanny yet incredibly powerful experience to unfold. Our art focalizer that week had noticed that, as a group, we were caught up in our own fears of not being good enough artists, hence were reluctant to begin our projects.

First, she talked about our inner critics, and how we were allowing this inner critic to stop us. Directed to find a place in front of a large (2-by-3 foot) sheet of black paper, we were invited to close our eyes while she led us in meditation.

Her voice helped us to breathe gently and deeply, her words guiding us on a journey. Finally, she led our visual imagery onto a train station platform, encouraging us to see a train arriving. Then through the steam of the engine, she suggested that our inner critic had stepped off the train and was coming through the steam toward us. She commanded us to open our eyes and draw as fast as we could - without thinking - just drawing the visage of this inner critic.

My hand flew across the paper, tossing down one color to grab another- not thinking, just drawing, slashing color onto the paper. In 7 minutes, I was done, and as I staggered back, the focalizer came immediately to me. When she saw my drawing, she gasped, then quickly handed me a piece of notebook paper and a pen.

"Write." she commanded. "Ask him questions. Do not think. Just ask, write the question, and let the answer come just as fast. DO NOT THINK ABOUT IT. Just do it. Write whatever he says, even if it does not make sense. Write."

I did as she said. The words just came. My hand wrote as fast as those words came, and no other thoughts intruded. When I was done, the focalizer stepped forward, read my words, then smiled, hugged me, and just walked away. I sat down on the floor and went to sleep. I was exhausted.

It wasn't until much later that I really looked at the picture and the words and thought about them. I felt that I'd just had one of the most profound conversations of my life.

Like the others in my group, I hung my Inner Critic in the Park Lecture Room where we displayed our art. However, after a few days, I noticed my drawing had been taken down. The four youngest women in our group were staying in rooms on the second floor of The Park Building. When I asked where my picture was, they told me they had taken it down because it scared them, that they often came into the Park Lecture Room to dance in the evenings, and they couldn't stand it watching them. So I took it back to my room.

Oddly enough, my son and others hate that picture and have tried to blame any bad luck they might think I had on that picture. They wanted me to destroy it, calling it a portrait of Lucifer. I refused for I didn't see it as evil; I saw it as 'sad and lonely'. To me, it was an inner part of me crying out to be loved, and I was refusing to deny it.

I am glad I did not destroy this picture, for when I recently took it out of the closet where it has been hidden so my family does not have to see it, I recognized once again how it is my own Inner Critic that fuels my thoughts with negativity.

Seeing the portrait again as I share this story - recognizing the grief again - I am reminded how important it is to acknowledge those feelings the Inner Critic creates, yet at the same time, to let them go.

Reading the words which I had taped to the back of the portrait remind me of my own shadow side who needs love also.

I see a lot of strength in this grief, the rigidity of survival, and the courage of facing this truth of me.

I did the gold edging more than 4 months later back in the USA ... at home.

My Inner Critic
by JanMarie Sajna
(Pastels on Black Paper)
2005 Findhorn Park, Scotland

Dialogue with My Inner Critic

Who are you? **I am Lucifer come to destroy you.**

Why do you want to destroy me? **Your light is too powerful; I must not let you speak.**

Of what are you afraid?
You humans having too much power.

Why are you wearing a clerical collar?
Because I can reach more people through the churches of this world.

At first your eyes looked wicked, now they just look sad. Why are you so sad?
Because God doesn't love me best.

Why is one of your ears distorted?
Because I cannot hear God loving me too.

Is that my fault?
No, I find my power in being unique so God not loving me gives me uniqueness.

But what if God does love you? What then?
I am just like everyone else.

Isn't that okay? **(no answer)**

Why are you burning? **I'm not burning, the fire is behind me.**

Why?
I want to burn away my past, my sorrow, my doubts, my fears, ... and be what God wants me to be.

How can I help you? **Love me**

One of the most difficult of the Fine Arts for me was Movement. When we began learning Bio-Dancing, I was hesitant, unsure, embarrassed, and tied up in knots. This kind of dancing encourages you to allow others to become very close to you, to enter your space, and for you to enter theirs. Oddly enough, the instruction to always look into each other's eyes was very hard at first. It was intimidating and full of vulnerability.

Sometimes one person would be chosen to be the center of the dance, and we would move closer to them until we were as one person with many arms and legs wrapped around each other, but without touching – an action of respecting space which has to be experienced to be understood. Movements were slow, steady, and so gentle. Everything was done with love, and we practiced giving as well as receiving that love. I hoped to be chosen to be center but feared it also. I was never chosen and experienced both regret and relief.

Our dance leader led us with her voice until our bodies were in harmony, one with the others. Sometimes we were given bright red long scarves and told to dance like the flames in a fire. She would tell us a story, and we would move to that story like fire becoming embers or perhaps blazing bonfires. Sometimes, we were prairie fires racing across fields - burning, lifting our arms in reaching flames, ducking down as wind swept through. We became fire. We became water. We became the wind. And we became the rain - until the fire sizzled out, leaving us prostrate on the floor.

I, who never ran, for my legs always hurt, for my tension always kept me tied up in knots - I ran, and I leapt, I spun and I flung my arms out like they were wings, and everyone cheered, for they knew how hard it was for me to let go and fly like that.

I danced the fire dance and felt my own perfection of movement. I bared my feet and bared my soul, running from the pain and the fear, barely able to breathe but fixing a rigid smile on my face and making myself move through the stiffness. Finally, I ran free ... kind of.

Prayers for a Healthy Body

I am in the flow of life, infused with God's restoring energy. Free of any stress, strain, or worry, I claim perfect health and wholeness. I deny any health condition or diagnosis having power over me. I know the truth of my being: that I am made in the image and likeness of God, and my body has the innate capacity to heal. The miracle of life works its wonders in me, and I am grateful.

Prayers for Healthy Thoughts

If my mind hears words or sounds that bring up feelings of worthlessness or criticism, the cleansing power of Spirit transforms this energy. Divine life present in every cell of my being infuses me with purifying light. With each cleansing, restoring breath I feel a deep sense of safety. As I forgive myself, rivers of divine love flow through me and peace washes over me. As I forgive, I accept myself and others just as they are. God is here and all is well. I am loved.

FOURTEEN

Pottery

Pottery began with Craig in a Native American rustic Hogan that had a fire pit in the middle. It was dark; the sun set around four in the afternoon, so night came early. Craig, who had been at Findhorn since its earliest days, told us he had gone out around 4 a.m. onto the flats of Findhorn Bay that morning to gather the clay that appeared when the tide went out. It was a black, wet clay. Gathered around the fire pit, we each accepted a handful of this very wet strange clay, and Craig told us to just warm it in our hands, knead it, and to listen as he told us a story.

His story was about the first people, about their lives in community, perhaps in a cave, perhaps a tent of sorts - cavemen times. He told us how these people, as they evolved, searched for meaning in the land, sea, and sky surrounding them. A natural storyteller, he told how they gathered the clay in their hands, and noticed that as it warmed it began to feel like flesh.

With his words, we suddenly realized that what we were holding had now warmed, and did indeed feel like flesh. "And he took clay and formed Man." Craig said.

He had us close our eyes. We sat around the fire listening to him talk quietly, as we explored the clay in our hands. He instructed us to let our fingers shape the clay into whatever called to us. Then he began to hum a familiar chant, a Native American song. Slowly we joined him, adding harmonies until the sound wrapped itself around us, transporting us into the far distant past - until we were there with the cavemen communing in our most basic humanity.

Then we opened our eyes to see what our hands had formed in the clay. What we saw is what you can see in museums of the earliest clay figures. Craig told us to set them into the edge of the fire, and should we choose to reach into the bucket and get more clay, to help ourselves.

Singing softly, we listened to one another, to the fire, and to our own deepest persona – shaping whatever we were drawn to create. Each person probably made at least three figures to harden in the fire. A photo of my first two are below (one lost her head in the fire):

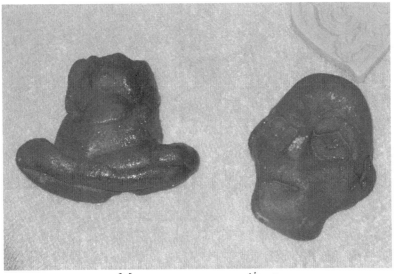

My cave-person creations

Craig was our introduction to working with clay, and The Pottery Shed became one of my favorite art places. This building which was much more than a shed, was warmed by a big old wood stove in the center of the room. There was a long table at which we all worked. Off to the side were throwing wheels, but I never used those.

*Georgette, Almut, Lesley, and Desie
Antonio, Camilla, Olivia, Robyn, Me, Zoe,
Martine*

Our other pottery focalizer, Belia, began by giving us a ball of clay about the size of a softball. Then she had us close our eyes as she led us on a guided imagery journey. At different points in her narrative, we were told to do specific things with the clay, to create a character or an object from the story - perhaps to shape the ball into something that simply cried out to be formed as we listened. This was hands-on meditation. We sat there listening to her voice and to the fire crackling in the cast iron stove for nearly an hour. Upon opening our eyes to see what we had made, lots of laughter and even surprise erupted. Some people had made very recognizable objects and we were amazed, especially those of us whose creations looked like nothing but blobs of clay.

Each of the fine arts was given a week of classes, so we spent a week of formal afternoons working with the clay, but many of us were hooked and came whenever we could spare the time to play in the Pottery Shed. Slowly, my figures took on shape and beauty. I discovered that molding the clay was difficult for my arthritic hands, but if I was able to manage approximate shapes, once the clay reached a leathery stage, I could carve the details with the various tools our focalizer provided.

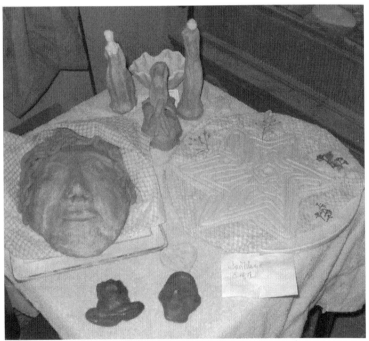

My favorite creations from the Pottery classes

Martine, Nigel, Olivia, Camilla, Jan, Almut and Antonio working in the Pottery shed.

Working with clay became a "coming home" kind of activity - coming home to me, to my creativity. I loved every minute of it, sitting there working while my feet warmed on the fender of the stove, taking a break for tea, warm bread and jam, and conversation. Sometimes we sang as we worked. I think everyone in the group felt the same lovely energy. Spending hours in silence, in humming, in soft harmonic singing, or in listening to classical music as we worked was like being in the safest home with the most wonderful people in the world.

Our group was given the opportunity to do a special project that would become a permanent fixture of Findhorn, both for the community to remember us and to give us a symbol of our involvement in community. We decided to create a beautiful staircase down a hill behind Cluny Hotel, an area so steep that steps had long been needed.

After much discussion, we enthusiastically all agreed when the suggestion came, that we would make it represent the Australian Rainbow Serpent using ceramic tiles, clay and porcelain chards, dragon's tears (small lima bean shaped glass pieces), marbles, and polished stones, etc.

First, we planned out the design on the floor of the ballroom at Cluny, and then went outside where a maintenance crew had dug out the area for the steps. Filling each blocked out step with cement, we then pressed our bits and pieces of bright colors into the wetness. It was quite cold as we worked, and damp as you can see in the photos. We didn't finish until after dark.

Martine and Jan

It is getting dark as we put the last touches on our Dreamtime Rainbow Serpent Staircase down the hill next to Cluny Hotel.

Prayers of Joy

As we go forth to do our work with ease, creativity, and efficiency, we are grateful for the joy and enthusiasm bubbling up from our hearts. We allow the love of God to flow through us to our co-workers, and all who come into our work area. We know that as love flows from us, it surely does return to us as peace, harmony, and goodwill.

Prayers of Blessings

The joy of the Lord is in us. Our Happiness comes from the love that fills our hearts. We give thanks for our growing awareness of the radiant Christ presence within us. We celebrate the work of our hands with joy and peace,. We give thanks for all we have experienced, and our hearts are filled with Divine Love

FIFTEEN

Music

Music was such an integral part of my stay at Findhorn that everything I did and everywhere I went was a song. Taize` singing became the beginning of every day, and I often went to sleep with one of the day's songs floating through my mind. Our group would break into song at any time, so music stayed with us through everything.

Each day, I rose a good hour before daybreak, dressed and walked in the dark to the Nature Sanctuary where anywhere from four to a dozen singers gathered to begin the day.

Nature Sanctuary

Inside of Nature Sanctuary

I was the only one of my Essence of the Arts group to sing

with the Taize` singers every day. People took turns leading, amazing singers who were able to teach and sing each harmony part. I was an alto then, but I was not musically confident enough to lead the group. It was all I could do to learn my alto part and the words each day.

Ian Turnbull, a long time Findhorn resident, had built the Nature Sanctuary by hand many years before. This Sanctuary had such wonderful acoustics that a group of four singer - an alto, a soprano, a tenor, and a bass - could sound like an entire choir.[10]

From the Nature Sanctuary, we went directly to the Main Sanctuary for group meditation, which drew 30 or more people every day. The Sanctuary was open for meditation all the time and I went whenever I could, but the morning meditation and the one just before dinner were group gatherings I never missed.

We sang songs and chants from many cultures and many lands. Native American songs and chants are very popular at Findhorn, for their spirituality and connection to the earth is highly respected by the environmentally conscious Findhorn residents.

Inside the Nature Sanctuary where Barbara Swetina had begun the custom of daily meditation through Taize` singing, people relaxed on cushions and carpet squares, often sitting Native American style in this magical place. [11]

---

[10] *https://www.findhorn.org/2012/08/a-circle-of-songs/*

[11] *CD's of Barbara's music, song books, and invitations for her to do workshops can be accessed through her website: (http://www.sacredsongs.net/)*

On Christmas Eve, beginning right after dinner, we gathered in the Sanctuary for an evening of song, meditation and prayer. People came and went all evening, some with musical instruments from around the world, yet the Sanctuary was always full. In candle light, Buddhists, Christians, agnostics, Catholics, Jews, and many other faiths joined their desires for peace, love, and joy into a gathering that truly celebrated the birth of a consciousness destined to change the world.

I stayed until the last of the singers left around 3:00 a.m., unable to leave the most spiritual, the most beautiful Christmas night I've ever experienced. I have no photographs of this night, for I was not there to take pictures, I was there to be a part of the magic.

The Park Building girls, Olivia, Camilla, Zoe and Martine put on a St. Lucia celebration for all of us near Christmas, which included a dinner and lots of caroling.

My friend Jan from Australia chose as her last project, to create a photographic essay of our time at Findhorn. Because cabbage is served at every meal and because the giant 40 pound cabbages were the thing that drew people to Findhorn when it first began its spiritual journey, Jan asked each of us to pose with a cabbage doing one of the things we loved the most at Findhorn.

Camilla & Cabbage Kids *Jan, Camera, & Cabbage*

I chose to sing Taize` with my cabbage in the Nature Sanctuary, as Music was so important to me.

My last day singing with the Taize` group was wonderful. That last day I finally had the musical courage to teach them my favorite song chant which goes like this:

"All I ask of you is forever to remember me as loving you.
(repeat)
"Ishk Allah ma bood li la, Ishk Allah ma bood li la"
(repeat)
(Arabic, meaning something like
"Love, Beloved, Lover, Loving)

"Kyrie" from "Songs of Heaven and Earth"
Songs of celebration from around the world
by Barbara Swetina and the Findhorn Singers 2001.
Printed with permission from Barbara Swetina.

Prayers for Happy Times

We rejoice with one another; we are truly blessed by God's presence in our lives. Each day is a new experience, and each need is fulfilled at the right time and way. We share in each other's joy in this blessing of singing together, celebrating together, and just being together, for God's life is my life, and I vibrate with music, harmony and wholeness.

Prayers for Blessings

The joy of the Lord is in you. Your happiness comes from the love that fills your heart. You give thanks for your growing awareness of the radiant Christ presence with you. You are so grateful to be a part of God's worldwide family.

Prayers for Healing

God's life and love flow within your mind and body as a steady stream of healing energy and strenghtening power. Your entire body is restored, and your heart and mind are at peace.

SIXTEEN

Conception

A group of us decided to take an evening doll-making class with our art teacher/focalizer at her home in Findhorn Village. She had a wonderful work room with a wide variety of fabric scraps and sewing supplies. It was such a joy to sit around her big table with the others, talking and laughing as we worked.

We would head out after dinner to walk in the starlight or mist along Findhorn Bay, a 20 to 30 minute walk to her little Scottish cottage. Some of us used this time for co-listening, arms linked in comradeship. Sometimes we sang.

The road to Findhorn Village

Findhorn Village street   My Doll

And sometimes we were quiet, just listening to our footsteps and the night as Findhorn Bay's small wavelets lapped at the rocky shore.

I wasn't particularly thinking about the doll I was making as we sat in fellowship around her table. I was more interested in the conversation so I was as surprised as everyone else when my doll began to take on the appearance of being a mother with a new baby. The others teased me sweetly about it being my hope for a grandchild, even though I told them my son and his lady weren't ready yet to start a family. Unconsciously I had even given the doll red hair like my son's lady, Adrienne.

A couple weeks later, having finished my doll, I started another one which was to be completed on the last evening of our class. That afternoon before heading to Findhorn Village, I decided to call my son because I hadn't talked with him for several weeks. Imagine my surprise when he told me they'd just found out that day that Adrienne was pregnant.

When I told him about the doll, he asked when I had added the baby to the doll. When I told him it was a Thursday, just three weeks previously, he laughed and said that was the same day and time when the baby was conceived. My doll making class was ecstatic, sure that I'd had a premonition from around the world, which wasn't all that surprising considering the unusual events surrounding Adam and Adrienne.

Here is their story: On Mother's Day at the turn of the Millennium, I was asked to do a storytelling at my church, Unitarian Universalist of Kansas City. I chose the story by Robert Munch, "I Will Love You Forever." After the service, in the greeting line, a woman about my age came up to me and took my hands. She was weeping, but she was also smiling.

"I've been fighting with my teenage son all week," she said. "We fought all night long. I couldn't stand being around him another minute so I got dressed and came to church. I haven't been here for months."

I smiled to encourage her to go on, for I'd learned that sometimes, my stories brought something to the surface for folks to be healed, and it was my job to facilitate that healing through listening.

"Your story put everything into perspective," she said. "Thank You." Her tears continued rolling down her cheeks, so I knew there was something else going on.

Stepping into what I call my listening-to-Spirit space, I found myself asking, "Do you have any other children?"

"I have a daughter who lives in Denver, "she replied.

"Oh," I answered. "My son lives in Boulder. How old is your daughter?"

When she answered "26," I immediately responded, "My son is 26." And a ball of light burst open in my lower right abdomen and shot up through my body and out the top of my head. I blinked in surprise and wonder, holding myself suspended between what was happening in my energy body, and what was happening there in the receiving line.

"Is she married?" I asked breathlessly.

"No," she said. "And it is a problem because she is very intelligent, and she needs a man who is also very intelligent, who has a dream, and who is not afraid to follow his dream."

"You just described my son," I said as another ball of light shot from my abdomen, the left side this time, up through my body and out the top of my head. My sense of awe increased right along with the wonder.

At that moment, time briefly stopped, and at the same moment, in tandem, we each spoke, one with the other.

She said,	I said.
"Her name is Adrienne.	*"His name is Adam.*
They have to meet."	*They have to meet."*

And the biggest ball of light so far erupted from my lower abdomen, shot straight up from my uterus through my body, and burst over my head like a Nova going off.

We were both stunned, even though Adrienne's mother did not experience the balls of light like I did. We traded phone numbers and email addresses, promising to contact our own kids to encourage them to meet.

Two vital important young people such as Adam and Adrienne really did not want their mothers attempting to fix them up. They kept blowing us off - "leave me alone, Mom, I can find my own dates!" is what we each heard. So one day we decided to blackmail them. We each let our kid know that we were planning to come out to Colorado in my motor home to make sure they met.

A bit panicked, Adrienne finally sent an email to Adam stating that perhaps they should meet just to get the mothers off their backs. He agreed, but being busy professionals, they had a great deal of difficulty finding a compatible time to meet. They ended up emailing each other all summer and found themselves being brutally honest in order to try to find a reason to tell the mothers why it would never work for them.

Adam came home over Labor Day weekend. After dinner, he pulled out a stack of emails an inch or more thick, and handed them to me. "Read a couple of these," he requested.

I read an email in which Adrienne had asked, "What is this about golf?" and my son had written such a wonderful response that for the first time I finally understood what a person's attraction to golf entailed. I looked at Adam, only to see a sheepish look on his face, and I thought, "He's falling in love with her."

"What if when I meet her, I'm not attracted to her?" He nervously asked.

"Well then," I said. "You'll know you've made a very good friend."

Adam flew out a couple of days later, heading for Salt Lake City on a business trip. He called me early on the following Saturday morning, minutes after returning to Boulder. "I have a message from Adrienne on my phone," he told me. "She says she's not going to write another word to me until we meet. What do I do?"

I could tell he was very nervous. "Take her to a park for a picnic." I instructed. "You bring the food. Then go for a walk and just talk. Then call me and tell me all about it." I had to remind him when he repeated his question about attraction to just accept that he'd found a good friend, so everything was in win-win status.

I waited for him to call all evening. I waited all day Sunday. Well, I didn't wait; I tried to call him several times. On Monday, I took my calling card to school and tried to call him on every break I had. No answer. I was really getting concerned ... fearing I had introduced my son to the only female serial killer on the face of the earth. I even called his work but they didn't know where he was either and were concerned because he never missed work, and he should have called.

Late Monday night, the phone rang. It was Adam. "I did what you said, Mom. I took a picnic, we went to a park, we ate lunch, and then we walked. We walked and we walked ... until seven this morning. I think we must have walked every street in Denver, and my shoes have holes in them. I only came home to get some clean clothes, and then I'm heading back down there."

I smiled. *My son is in love* was my thought.

Then he asked, almost wistfully. "Mom, have you ever heard of this? When she's talking, her eyes will change from deep green to dark blue right when I am looking into them."

I didn't need to answer for he already knew what he knew. In 2010, they had twin boys who are the loves of my life.

This was not the first time I'd known ahead of time about a child ready to come into this plane of existence. Thirty two years before the making of the doll in Findhorn Village, on the day before Thanksgiving in 1973, a small child had appeared to me in a bowling alley in Overland Park, Kansas.

I'd been in the hospital for three days where tests were being run to try to find out why I was having blackouts. I wouldn't lose consciousness completely because sometimes these spells happened while I was driving, but I would lose periods of time - miles of time. That Wednesday, they'd done the brain wave test as well as a blood sugar test, so I was feeling very yucky. My waist length hair was goopy from the paste they'd used for the brain wave test, and all I wanted was to go home and wash my hair.

I had let my husband know that I would be released at noon, but he didn't show up. I waited for hours, so embarrassed by the compassion of the nurses as they tried to make me feel better about being left there. My husband did not show up until after 7 p.m. even though I had called him many times. He was very annoyed at having to leave work, and I was horrified to discover we seemed to be heading back to his work instead of home.

Across the street from the car dealership where he worked was a huge bowling alley. He pulled up to the front doors, handed me a five dollar bill, and told me to get out, that he would be back to pick me up when the dealership closed at 10 p.m. He gave me a shove to get me moving out of the car. I felt terrible, emotionally and physically, as I walked into the bowling alley with slow steps and head hanging in embarrassment at my hair full of paste and depression.

As I walked in, I saw only one group bowling. Down the center of the facility was a restaurant with tall wrought iron bars serving as open walls. On one side, the patrons could watch the bowlers, and on the other side, they could have watched ice skaters if there had been any there that night. The ice skating rink was dark.

I went into the restaurant and chose a table right next to the bars on the bowling alley side. This table was hidden from the bowlers though, because there were two vending machines on the other side of the wrought iron wall, with about 18 inches of space between them. A recessed light in the ceiling shone into that space.

I wrote my order on a napkin because I was afraid I would burst into tears if I looked at anyone. When the waitress came, I just handed the napkin to her without raising my head. Then I leaned down to reach into my purse on the floor to get my cigarettes.

As I pulled one from the packet, I straightened back up while bringing the cigarette to my lips. That's when I saw a child watching me from between the two vending machines on the other side of the open wrought iron wall.

Clasping the bars, this child with a Buster Brown haircut and navy blue turtleneck, looked to be between two and three years old. I couldn't tell if it was a boy or a girl.

The child spoke ... and I broke apart into three people:

1. That part of me that is always able to put on a cheery face and demeanor for a child.

2. That part of me curled in a despair-filled fetal position.

3. That part of me that was just watching the whole scene.

The child said, **"You're in jail."**

I said (playing the game of the bars being jail bars)**, "No I am not, you are."**

The child, looking all around, spoke again, **"The whole world's in jail."**

I asked, **"Who's going to let us out?"**

The child looked at me with a very matter of fact manner. **"God will."**

From my mouth came the words, **"Who's going to ask Him for the key?"**

The child, head cocked to the side, then leaning back in thought for a moment, and finally with a big beautiful smile as he leaned toward me again, said, **"I will ask God for the key to let you out."**

At that instant, it was like a million pounds had been lifted from my shoulders – I was stunned by the freedom! Then I realized that the child was gone. Disappeared. Evaporated. I rose and ran to look for the child, figuring that such a tiny child who spoke so well would be easily noticed. I could not find him – even asked several people if they'd seen him.

None had. Then I began wondering if I'd had a vision.

I told many people about this child during the next couple of months. Then on February 10, 1974 I conceived, and the whole incident left my memory completely. I was pregnant, and I was thrilled.

Almost exactly three years later: I was having lunch at the same bowling alley with my son who was 28 months old. We were on the side of the restaurant that faced the ice rink. In a weekly bowling league with my neighbor girlfriend, we often had lunch with our kids after league play. She had not come that day because one of her kids was sick, but I decided Adam and I would have lunch as we usually did. It was a very nice time. He was in the mood to talk quietly with mamma.

Then he dropped his toy car through the bars where I could not reach it, so telling him to stay right there, I went around the wall to get it. Bending over, retrieving it, I stood up and saw my son standing on his chair, clasping the bars, Buster Brown haircut, navy blue turtleneck, and watching me through the bars. He said, "God Bless You, Mom.", and instantly I realized he was the child I had seen three years before. He was small for his age and spoke very well. His haircut was exactly the same. It was the same child.

I was trembling as I went back around the wall and took him into my arms. Cupping his little hands around my face, he smiled and whispered, "I love you mommy."

I did not tell my son this story until he was 21 years old. He listened very quietly, then commented. "Mom, I can't tell you that I remember this, but I can tell you that I know it is true."

The day my grandsons were born, my son had called me to

tell me the birth was imminent. He'd stepped out into the hall for just a moment as they prepped Adrienne for the natural birth of twins, a delivery which few hospitals permit, and fewer obstetricians are willing to undertake. I immediately went out to my Labyrinth to pray for an easy, quick delivery. As I went into a meditation while sitting on the bench in the center of the labyrinth, I was blessed to see, when I closed my eyes, my twin grandsons as young men, standing at the entrance to the Labyrinth.

Mason was slightly taller than Alex. They were dressed in dark suits with white shirts, no ties, hands in their pockets, grinning at me. They looked like their dad at twenty-one, slim and very handsome. When Adam called me back to report their birth, he said that the doctor told them it was the easiest birth of twins he'd ever seen. Adam said, "They just slipped right out. Thanks mom for the prayers."

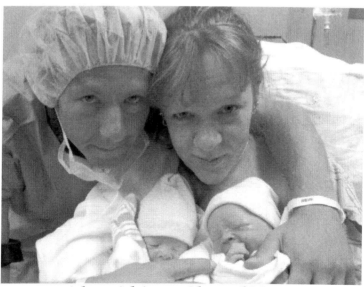

Adam, Adrienne, Alex and Mason

Prayers for Children (Maternity)

The Christ presence within fills you with light, life and strength. Your mind and body work together harmoniously for your total well-being and for the perfect development of the new life within you. You are strengthened and radiantly happy as you nurture the new life developing within you. You have faith that both your baby and you are enfolded in God's love and you are blessed with perfect health.

Prayers for Birth of a Child

The arrival of a new soul is a precious gift of life. God's richest blessing enfolds little _____, and (He/she) is filled with light, love, and joy. God's wisdom guides you in your role in this beloved child's life. _____ is divinely nurtured and protected today and always.

SEVENTEEN

Christmas Miracles

Many of my group traveled or went home over the Christmas holiday break when we had no meetings, however I stayed. One evening during dinner, a young couple entered and rang the bell for attention which was the accepted way to make announcements in the big community dining room. They told us they needed help.

They were Buddhists and had recently bought the magnificent mansion down the road, and were in the process of turning it into the Shambala-Retreat-Center.[12] Long time residents seemed to know them well. They announced that the trucks carrying their 40 new beds had just arrived, and they were requesting volunteers to help unload, unpack, and set them up. Along with about 30 others, I walked over to help. With no meetings, I was looking for something to do, and it sounded like fun.

The building was beautiful, a bit shabby as old mansions go, but still regal and exciting. Everyone helped with the

---

[12] See: http://www.findhorn.com/nfa/Organisations/ShambalaRetreatCentre

unloading, unpacking, and arranging of beds. Lots of laughter and even happy prayer over the beds ensued. Before we left, they asked for volunteers to come back during the next couple of days to help get the rooms ready for their first retreat, which was scheduled to occur in just three days.

Along with many others, I went. I washed windows, cleaned out fireplaces, dusted carved wood doors and trim, cleaned bathrooms, and sheeted beds.

Shambala Retreat Center on Findhorn Bay

Washing a huge window in one of the bedrooms, I noticed a walking prayer labyrinth at the edge of the extensive lawns of the mansion, so during my break, I went to walk in prayer. The energy of that labyrinth was of such sweet peace, I knew I would return. As usual when encountering a labyrinth away from home, I prayed to connect its energy to mine back in Missouri.

The young couple was so grateful for our help, they promised us a special night of music and sacred dance in the ballroom after the retreat was done. A couple days after Christmas, everyone walked over to Shambala. Along with the young couple who were also very talented musicians and singers,

Barbara Swetina led the group in Sacred Music and Dance. There were probably a hundred people dancing.

Sacred music and dance is a slow group meditation and time of prayer using beautiful chanted songs, often Native American songs, and prayer songs from all over the world. With the words, we were taught movements that helped us to enter an energy flow that was like drifting down the most beautiful stream of light: gentle, sweet, and full of love. The purpose to which we all agreed for the evening at Shambala was that we would send our love and our prayers for peace out to the world.

We gathered in the mansion's ballroom, which had many large windows looking out over Findhorn Bay. Deep into the evening, we danced and we sang, moving together in harmony of body, mind, and spirit.

There came a time, when Barbara asked all the men to form an inner circle around the musicians. So far we had been dancing in a big outer circle through many songs. For this song, the women were on the outer circle. Our male host led the men in singing "The Earth is Our Mother … We must take care of her." in their deepest voices. Barbara Swetina led the women on the outside ring as we sang "Ave Maria." And the sound had texture, warmth, coolness, and flow. It was gentle yet powerful and exquisitely real.

Our dance movements had us reaching into the inner circle with our hands and hearts, to scoop up all the love we felt there, and to gracefully carry it in our arms in a movement that had us sending it out the ballroom windows, out over Findhorn Bay, and into the night sky as we sang. I don't know how many times we did this movement and sang those verses. I do know that the harmonies and the movement became one of the most incredible experiences of my life.

At one point when I was closest to the bay side of the ballroom, as I reached into the center of the group, I could actually feel the energy in my hands, and then in my arms .... And I began to feel it sliding out of my hands and arms as I offered it to the world. I continued feeling this wonderful sensation all through my next traverse around the room. Reaching the same area where I first noticed the feeling, I discovered I could now see the energy also.

It was iridescent, opalescent-like, white with sparkles of all colors moving through it. I watched myself gather it as though I was gathering a gossamer fabric, felt and saw it against my heart and chest, and watched it slide down my arms and out of my hands, soaring out over the Bay and then swooping up into the sky to spread out like the most amazing fireworks, except it didn't fade out. It continued on until it was out of sight. I could see this light energy coming not just from me, but from all the others, swooping out over the water in waves. We had been singing and dancing for a long time, yet time ceased on this one prayer-song, for we were all in the most wonderful harmony of movement, mind, heart, and music.

Later, after midnight, as we walked alone or in small groups back to Findhorn Park, some were quiet like me, and some were talking in hushed voices. As I walked alone and listening, I heard several different people remark about how they began to see the energy just like I had seen it, even using similar words to what I've used here to try to describe this amazing magic. The gratitude I felt to have been part of this evening was profound.

Various groups met in the Sanctuary at Findhorn for prayers for beloved causes, especially at Christmas. One group I joined over the holiday was praying for peace in all countries. Each person was given a card engraved with the name of the country and its flag as they entered. Left over cards were passed out before we began praying, so people might be holding up to five or ten cards. A large map was spread on the floor. As each country was named, the person holding the card would place it on the world map. Then we would affirm peace, something like this: "We see Peace for Cambodia ... We see peace for Canada," etc. Once all the countries were placed, we would enter the silence of guided meditation.

One evening while meditating with this group, I had a vision of the earth with many groups like ours praying. I saw the energy of their prayers wafting upward and being gathered into a beautiful chalice. As the Chalice filled, the energy began spilling over its sides to rain down upon the earth with a power and beauty so much stronger than the individual prayer wisps which had entered it in the first place. It was such a powerful vision that when I left the Sanctuary, I went straight to the Park Building, got out my art supplies, and drew what I had seen.

The following week, before people began gathering for the "Pray for Peace" meditation, I took this singular chalice picture to the Sanctuary and tacked it onto the wall next to the entrance door. Because I was curious what people would think, I sat down and took a very long time removing my shoes, coat and scarf so I could hear what they might say. I wasn't surprised, yet I *was* surprised at how many people commented that this was exactly the Vision they had while meditating with the group. They were delighted to have their own visions confirmed, as was I.

Prayer Vision

That week between Christmas and New Year's was a quiet contemplative time for my heart and my art. Being shy about my art, I was hesitant to draw when others were near, but having the Park Building art room to myself that week, I was able to immerse myself in visioning and creativity. In that quiet time, I created a Mandala of my vision.

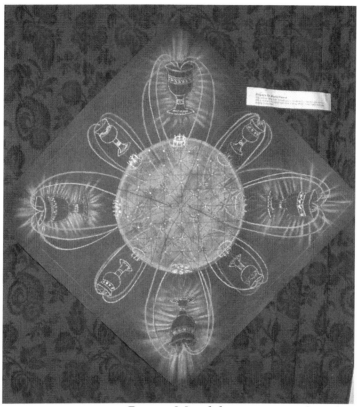

Prayer Mandala

When not drawing, I was walking the dunes to the North Sea, meditating in the woods, in the Main Sanctuary, in the Nature Sanctuary. Wherever I found myself ... I was in constant prayer. Fed by my aching heart over the strange rejection by Robyn, my week of solitude before falling onto my head was a beautiful time, and I was becoming comfortable in my aloneness, ... yet that injurious fall forced me out of my solitude and back into the group when I could not manage on my own.

In so many ways, I felt so blessed to be at Findhorn, but on

New Year's Eve at nine o'clock in the morning; I slipped and fell on an icy stone ramp. I fell onto the back of my head as if a giant had grabbed my feet, and like snapping a wet towel, this imaginary giant slammed my head down as hard as he could.

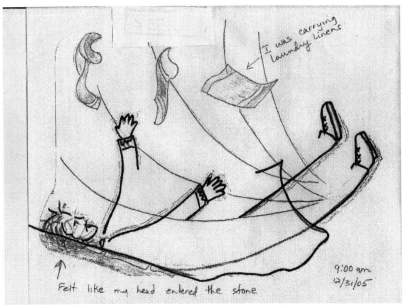

The sketch I made to show the doctor the anatomy of the fall.

From inside the guest lodge, Antonio heard the terrible sound my head made when it hit the stone ramp and hurried out still carrying the towel he'd been using to dry the dishes. When I tried to raise up, it was as if all the world was in a mirror, and that mirror had shattered ... with each piece of the mirror spinning, and between the many broken pieces was a *nothingness* that was horrifying.

I screamed in terror and covered my eyes, crying while Antonio held the towel to my bleeding head until the paramedics arrived. Others brought blankets to cover me for I could not raise up from the pain in my head. I had to ask the paramedics to keep my eyes covered for the ride to the hospital. Continuing to see the spinning pieces of shattered mirror left me distraught.

I ended up in the hospital twice in Scotland. The severe concussion left me so dizzy; I could not walk alone for weeks. I had a brain concussion as well as an inner ear concussion. My last month at Findhorn was one of pain, despair, confusion, and weakness. "Why??" is a question I continued to ask myself for several more years? "Why did this happen during the trip of my life?"

The most constant consequence of my injury was that I had to always be completely in the NOW, in the present moment. I had to concentrate so strongly on the area within a circle about 3 feet in diameter surrounding me. If I thought or looked past this 3 feet, I became so dizzy that I would begin to tip over. I could not look at people walking by, for their movement was more visual stimulation than I could tolerate. Noise bothered me the same way. I found it very difficult and tiring to try to follow a conversation.

For most of the month of January, I was only able to watch my group. I could not participate, and often had to lie down during many afternoons to rest.

One day during a nap, I began running a fever, which sent me into such terrible dizziness that I could not move. Feeling like I would be flung off the bed with the spinning, my hands gripped my blankets as I cried out for someone to come. I could hear Robyn talking on her cell-phone down the hall, so I began to call for her. As far as I knew, she was the only one in the building with me. I was so dizzy, it was extremely difficult to even make a sound other than weeping.

Finally, my door opened and Nigel entered with Robyn behind him. I was crying in terror of the horrendous spinning. Robyn stayed with me while he ran to get our focalizers. Robyn is a nurse, so she knew to lay her hands on my back with sufficient pressure to give me a sense of security. In spite of her hatred for me, she stepped up to the plate to help me when I needed it, and I was very grateful.

Georgette and her husband took me to the hospital right away, where I stayed for several days while they tried to figure out what was exacerbating the vertigo. It turned out that I had a kidney infection which gave me fever, and a fever with concussion is not a nice combination because fever causes the brain to swell.[13]

Robyn helped me as she allowed her nurse's instincts to take over, so when I returned from the hospital, I asked her if we could talk. We had to wait until she was ready, which occurred the last week we were in Findhorn. At that time, she told me that I reminded her of her ex, who had betrayed her.

13

These vertigo and disorientation problems continued to plague me when I returned to the states. With the help of my sister, Launi, who had researched my symptoms, we learned that the brain concussion was not the only problem. The crystals in the labyrinth of my inner ears had shattered and broken off. They were floating in my balance center, causing the severe dizziness. Her research led us to a doctor who knew how to trap the crystals into the inner part of the labyrinth inside my ears. It is a miserable experience to go through but the Epley Maneuver, as it is called, helped tremendously. The dizziness decreased by about 80%. Gradually through the next few years, physical therapy improved my balance so much that I am almost back to 100%. {Interesting that it was a Labyrinth problem. Interesting also how this accident led to an incredible healing revelation a few years later; a story told in the chapters about Holos University}

Robyn never apologized, but as I listened to her speak, I knew this was all about her, that what she was going through had nothing to do with me, even though I was deeply affected by her hatred of me. I knew I had done my best to always be kind, to be understanding and compassionate, but as a result of her animosity toward me, I had allowed myself to become withdrawn from the group and very solitary. The injury forced me to leave my solitude and be dependent on others in the group.

Because of this experience with Robyn, I was able in later years to understand when someone else inexplicably shut me out of her life. Understanding allowed me to step away from the hurt, and remain neutral in that situation as I allowed compassion to keep me level and serene.

Prayers for World Peace

As we pray for World Peace, we become aware that peace begins with each individual. Our peaceful thoughts, words, and actions reach out from us to every woman, man and child – and to every country in the world. Peace radiates from the hearts of all pelple and touches the world. God's Spirit within gives all people the desire to live in peace and harmony. We envision people of all races and nationalities joining together to create a world that is safe, filled with love and understanding, where every need is abundantly met.

Prayers for Divine Order

In prayer you now release all fears concerning this situation. You totally trust God to be in Charge. As you wait you are at peace, knowing God's Holy Spirit is bringing forth a divine solution.

Prayers for Healing of the Mind

God's healing energy fills your mind. The healing love of God flows through you. You are relaxed – free in mind and spirit. Whenever any disturbing thoughts or feelings arise within you, they come to be healed.. Thank God for this awareness and that divine love heals you in every way. Your emotions are calm, and your mind and body are revitalized, strengthened, and renewed.

EIGHTEEN

Findhorn Puzzles

"The Saint Germain Puzzle"

This narrative so far has been lacking in interpretation to a certain extent, leaving it up to the reader to make their own conclusions. I have stated the feelings associated with the events because I thought it important to report reactions. Some of those reactions are still puzzling to me; others make sense in relation to lifelong experiences and hindsight. The next part of this story has been a puzzle and still is unsolved.

My concussion made life very difficult. I wasn't able to do very much, but I still wanted to take part in the final show scheduled for January 20, 2006. This show was the culmination of our three months in the Essence of the Arts Programme. I planned to perform a storytelling of a children's book I had written while there. The performance included the song, "Sixteen Tons" as well as the drawings I'd done for the children's book I'd written, which would be projected onto the screen above me as I told the story.

I thought I could do it if I sat in my chair and told the story without my usual storyteller élan. I would tell the story quietly and let the pictures and the imagination of the audience fill in what I could not evoke through my style and flair as the storyteller.

Two days before the big performance, we were going through the entire show. When it was my turn, Jan and Camilla helped me to my chair, and I began my story. By the time I reached the end, I was so dizzy, so faint, and so disoriented; I could not stand by myself, and was even having trouble staying upright in my chair. I had to be taken back to my room by two members of the group to lie down.

The next morning, I awoke, and as I lay there in the dark, I had a vision. I knew it was a vision as compared to a dream because it was so real, and because I was also aware that I was lying in my bed. I saw myself sitting in my chair on the night of the performance. I was telling my story. When I finished, the audience was applauding and cheering, but I was slowly falling from the chair. I saw my soul rise up from my body and hover high above everyone. I watched folks run to me and begin working over my body. I knew I had died, and I also knew I had a choice to make.

The vision ended, and I was left with the choice. Should I take this opportunity to die, or should I choose to live? I saw this in the terms that I would die if I performed. I rose from my bed and carefully made my way to the kitchen of the guest lodge where I was staying. I could walk alone if I kept my hands on the wall and went very slowly. I wrote down the vision, then I sadly made the choice to NOT perform. I wanted to perform but more than that, I wanted to live. I also knew I could not talk about this without crying, so I wrote a letter to the group telling them of the vision and of my decision.

My friend and co-listener, Jan, came into the kitchen and seeing my distress as I handed her the pages, silently read what I'd written. She asked if I wanted her to read the letter to the group. All I could do was very carefully nod.

Jan read the letter. The group was shocked but also respectful of my decision. They did ask if I thought I could still play my Native American flute in the group song as it had an integral part in the piece. It was decided that I would sit on a bench to the side of the stage throughout the show in order to honor my participation, and then when the song came, two of the group would help me join the group for that portion of the show. Everyone at Findhorn knew of my concussion and my disability, so everyone understood.

To this day, I wonder what would have happened had I done my story. I wonder if my interpretation of the vision was correct or not. At the time, I wasn't willing to take the chance that it would mean my death.

A few weeks before falling on my head, another issue with storytelling occurred in a little café perched on a small hill at Findhorn where community members gather sometimes for an Open Mic night. A Storytelling Evening was advertized, so I decided to go. I'd been a professional storyteller at one time, but I had gradually let that part-time interest slide as it was such a lonely activity for me. I was very good at it, and enjoyed performing, but the many, many hours of lonely practice before each performance just didn't seem worth the short accolades.

Perhaps it was my desire to be accepted that encouraged me to sign up to tell a story one Friday night. Some of my group was there but my shyness and the need to review my story in my mind led me to sit alone.

I noticed as I watched that the storytellers who got the most applause were actually the worst ones. I began to realize that the audience was applauding their courage, not their ability. Not sure what to do, my name was called before I could make a decision on whether to perform or not, so taking a deep breath; I rose and went to the stage.

The story I told was one of my best, an African creation myth called "A Story, A Story," one that was a favorite of my audiences, one I was very comfortable doing. The applause was scant, short, and faint. They were just not interested. Returning to my seat, I stayed through three more stories that were terrible, but I applauded the teller's courage with big smiles and shining eyes.

As soon as it felt appropriate, I rose and made my way outside to walk back to my room in the dark lonely night. I'd failed again, and even though I'd given myself a good reason, I still knew I had failed. I continued walking for hours, to Findhorn Village and back, through various paths in the Park … just walking, just breathing … and wishing I could cry.

One day in early December, I was in the Phoenix, the small general/grocery store at the entrance to Findhorn Garden. Hearing an American voice in the next aisle, I stepped around the display and greeted the lady standing there.
"American?" I asked.

"American," she replied. "I'm Jana."

We exchanged pleasantries about our reasons for being at Findhorn. It seems she had inherited a substantial amount of money from an aunt, and was traveling the world visiting various spiritual centers. She told me she'd come to Findhorn in her journey of following Spirit. I never met anyone who did that so I was very interested in hearing her story. We agreed to look for each other in the Community Center at dinner, promising to sit together.

Just as we were turning away to go about our business in the store, she stopped and put her hand on my arm. With an attitude of listening, she scrunched her eyebrows then looked at me closely. "Something or someone just told me to tell you that you are to go to Mt. Shasta," she said. "We can talk about it at dinner," she added.

"Whoa!" I thought.

We did. I told her everything that had happened concerning Mt. Shasta and St. Germaine. We both marveled at the voice she'd heard telling her the message to give to me. Jana left for India about a week later.

The one Royal Air Force Base (RAF) in the British Isles which has clear skies at some point each day is located at Findhorn. All other RAF Bases are often buried in fog or rain for days on end. Standing in the dunes or on the edge of the sea, you can see a very definite circle of clouds around this area. I am guessing it may be some 30 miles in diameter. The RAF Base was in its center.

The sun is always able to get through at Findhorn. I loved to stand on a high dune and turn slowly in a circle marveling at the rainbow colors in this halo of cloud reflected onto the water and even into the air, so I felt I was in the midst of a rainbow being incredibly blessed.

I found another labyrinth at Findhorn, one in the sand dunes among the gorse, cleansed by winds off the North Sea. The sky and sea at Findhorn was like liquid rainbow. The energy there was unique in my life experience.

The Stone Labyrinth looking to the North Sea and the bank of colorful clouds that often encircle the RAF Base and Findhorn.

Three days before I left Findhorn, I was told there was a message for me on the Community Bulletin Board. The girl who was supposed to have sanded the icy walkway upon which I'd fallen, had taken it upon herself to help me with whatever I needed while I was unable to do so much. She would check in with me each morning to attend to any of my needs. She retrieved the note for me, and I read:

JanMarie,

Please come to the office tomorrow (Thursday) between 9 and noon. I have a gift for you. Ask for Barbara.

I did not know a Barbara at Findhorn. Puzzled but curious and always ready for mystery, with my aide's help, I went to the office as instructed and asked for Barbara. A tall lady came forward holding a bag with something in it. She smiled and said. "When I was in the States on vacation last summer, I was in a Gift Shop buying gifts for friends here at Findhorn. As I stood at the counter to pay for my four items, a voice in my head told me to buy one more and that I would know who it was for when I saw *her*."

Barbara then told me how she usually didn't eat in the Community Center but had come for a birthday party there a few days previously. While there, she had looked across the room and seen me. Immediately she knew the item she had bought in the states was for me. She told me how she had asked around to find out who I was. Then she handed me the bag. "This is for you," she said.

I opened it, and experienced a rush of skin prickles. It was a calendar and each month's image was a different photograph of Mt. Shasta. Seeing my distress, she laid her hand on my arm, and said. "I think you know that you are supposed to go there. It's okay. You can go there."

In some ways, my stay at Findhorn was the trip of a lifetime. In others, it was a nightmare. I reached incredible heights and terrible depths there. My art recorded some of those moments. I learned to pray and to meditate in new ways, with a sensitivity that I hold with me today.

I left Findhorn, traveling back to the U.S. with the aid of a wheelchair to combat my terrible dizziness. Still having to cover my eyes from too much movement, everyone was very kind and helpful on my journey.

Prayers for Divine Order

You trust in God, knowing that whatever you do, wherever you go, God is the wisdom that guides, the power that governs, the love that blesses, the presence that protects, and the substance that prospers you. As you move forward this perfect order is established.

Prayers for Safe Travel

The Christ presence within you ensures your happiness and protection wherever you go. You believe in God's goodness, and expect the best to come forth. You rely on God's power to provide an abundance of all things needed for a safe and joyful journey.

Prayers for Protection

When you feel threatened, you remind yourself that the presence and power of God is all there is. Nothing can stand against God, There is no other power. You focus on God, and know that God is mightier than any circumstance. You are always divinely protected.

Part Three

Back in the USA

NINETEEN

Ahria and Angels

In April of 2006, a young woman named Ahria, came to my new church, Unity of Independence, and performed her music. She is a contemporary/new-thought singer and composer who performs at spiritual centers and consciousness events across the country.[14]

Across the crowded room after that Sunday service, our eyes met, and we both knew we needed to get together. I waited until she was finished meeting and talking with those who had lined up to thank her for her music. She came straight to me. We talked briefly, acknowledging that we both felt the draw that said we must get together and talk. I made arrangements to pick her up the next day.

I brought Ahria to my house. We walked the Labyrinth together. We shared stories of our lives. Once again, out of the blue came the words: "You must go to Mt. Shasta."

---

[14] *Ahria is also a practicing Urban Shaman trained by The Four Winds Society. She sees clients in the greater San Diego area and is also available for phone sessions. Contact her at* ahriasings@gmail.com.

I told Ahria the stories of the odd appearances and references to Mt. Shasta and St. Germaine that I had experienced all through my life, culminating with the incidents in Scotland.

Ahria, like Craig at Findhorn Garden, was very familiar with Saint Germain. She also lamented that I must have been sent a book about him authored by someone who was more hopeful of contact than someone who was actually in contact with Saint Germain. "He's an Ascended Master." she told me, and you need to go to Mt. Shasta to search for him.

I took Ahria on a tour of my house. As we climbed the stairs to the third floor, she suddenly staggered and almost fell. I was behind her, and steadied her until she was able to continue. It appeared that she was not ready to share what had happened to make her stagger, but I noticed that she was uncomfortable. Though puzzled at her odd expression, I went ahead and told her the story of the African American lady's visit and her visions. Ahria was very interested yet at the same time, I felt that something was bothering her a great deal. I saw that she held onto the railing very carefully as we went back downstairs.

Finally, I just asked her what had happened. She told me that she had hit a layer of energy that was terribly scattered and broken. "Shattered" was the word she finally chose. She went on to describe how she had encountered energy like this before in California in a house where people had been doing drugs. She shared her observations that hallucinogenic drugs were very destructive to a person's energy field, shattering it so that pieces were lost and often remained in the area where the drugs had been done.

Ahria had no way of knowing that the people who had been renting the house when I bought it had been doing drugs.

Two of the reasons the house was even at a price I could afford was because these renters had trashed the house, and because the neighbors had complained continuously about their erratic behaviors. Drugs had not been manufactured here but they had been used and sold from this house. Ahria had no way of knowing this, but her sensitivity had picked up on it anyway. I went on to share with Ahria some of the stories of odd occurrences in my house.

In the years since I had bought the house, many things had happened that had caused me to invite various folks to help with cleansing the house through prayer, smudging,[15] and various psychic interventions. At one point, I had to engage a well known psychic to do a cleansing because whoever was haunting the house was becoming a problem.

These entities had for the most part been helpful to me by aiding me in finding a lost pair of earrings through causing a vase to vibrate loudly until my investigation of the noise allowed me to find the earrings behind a small ceramic box which sat in front of the vase. Another helpful incident occurred when I was attaching a piece of wallboard to the ceiling of my walk-in closet. I leaned too far backwards and began to fall when suddenly, I felt a hand in the middle of my back catching and pushing me upright again. Startled, I mumbled my thanks and asked who it was. "Michael" was the answer I heard.

---

[15] *Mystics say the Native American practice of smudging, or purifying a room with the smoke of sacred herbs, can help clear negative energy from a space. And the apparent benefits are steeped in science – when burned, sage and other herbs release negative ions, which research has linked to a more positive mood. http://spiritualityhealth.com/articles/ancient-art-smudging*

The most helpful encounter occurred in the middle of the night when my Carriage House tenant called me to exclaim that two men were trying to break into my back door. "Call 911" I told her as I rushed to get dressed.

She called me back, and teasingly said, "Your boyfriend just chased them off. He's a pretty big fellow. I didn't know you had a boyfriend."

"What are you talking about?" I cried as I made my way downstairs, turning on the lights. I heard her gasp as the kitchen light went on, which would completely illuminate whomever she was seeing.

"He's gone." She cried, "and the burglars are running like they've seen a ghost". It wasn't long before the police arrived but it was too late to catch the two would-be thieves.

{Interestingly enough, upon relating this story of my Guardian Angel to insurance agents, I have qualified for a deduction for having an alarm system. This deduction was even given by more than one company.}

The trouble with these spirits or entities had begun when I started to sense that someone was dreaming through me, and that was plain creepy. I hated that terrible feeling of 'wrongness' that invaded my being.

Waking in the middle of night, I would call on Jesus to chase those entities out of my house. I would yell at them to "GET OUT" of my body, and to "GET OUT" of my house. After awhile, I moved to the Lavender Room, {the rooms in my house are named} but within two months, they'd found me there. Then I moved to my motor home, but after six weeks of that, I was seriously annoyed. At that time, I was seeing a psychologist, and was hesitant to tell her about these problems. When I finally did tell her, she recommended I call a particular psychic she knew who was very good at getting entities to move on.

Betty Lloyd, the recommended psychic, came to my house for a day in the late 1990's. She told me that a man and two women were here, and they loved what I was doing to the house, but they didn't understand about "moving on". She helped them to let go, to see the tunnel, and to go through it. Then she did a cleansing of the house and of me, teaching me prayers to protect myself from these kinds of events. (Note: I did find out later that a Doctor, his wife and his sister had lived here for decades. They were very strong Mormons ... which explained why I constantly had Mormons at my door wanting to convert me. After the cleansing, that stopped also.)

The atmosphere of the house had changed dramatically after Betty's cleansing rituals, and I had thought it was clear of the negative influences of its hundred-year existence. Ahria helped me to realize that I was wrong, and through her directions was able to complete the cleansing. After the cleansing Ahria recommended, I easily recognized the difference as did other family members who had sensed something but were unable to define their unease in words.

Per Ahria's instructions, I began to prepare myself for the cleansing ritual. Knowing that I needed to be out of the house for awhile, I moved into my motor home. I walked the Labyrinth every day, prayed and meditated, waiting until the right moment. I thought I would be required to consciously imagine each step as I worked through it. As it turned out, *I watched it happening in my mind's eye, a kind of vision in which I was an equal participant but not the director.*

On a Sunday morning, just a few weeks after the meeting with Ahria, I awoke in the motor home just before daybreak. As I lay there, the certainty that today was the day enshrouded me like a warm blanket. I rose, dressed, did my morning's ablations, and walked to the Labyrinth.

Ahria had told me that I was to invite three helpers from the spirit realm. I had not been able to figure out who to invite, so when I entered the Labyrinth, I walked in gratitude for whoever would come to help, welcoming those entities, those spirits whose interest and power would fit the bill, but I was still unable to name even one.

I reached the center of the Labyrinth, and turning to the southwest corner, I placed myself there in my mind's eye. Then I turned slowly to the southeast corner and as I turned, I searched my brain thinking *whom should I ask?* Nothing and no one came to mind, so I was astonished when I focused my attention onto that corner, astonished to see (in my mind's eye) that Michael the Archangel stood there. He winked at me in greeting. Delighted and surprised, I thanked him for coming. Somehow, I just knew who he was - no imagining was needed, he was just there and grinning at me.

Continuing in a circle, I turned until I was facing the Northeast corner, still wondering who would come, who would be there. When I saw him, I immediately knew it was Gabriel. Putting his fingers and palms together, he bowed to me in a Namaste greeting[16]. Again delighted and surprised, I thanked him for coming.

---

[16] *https://en.wikipedia.org/wiki/Namaste*

As my circle continued, I laughed at myself to realize I still couldn't think of the names of any other angels, so was really curious who would be in the Northwest corner. Immediately an angel appeared, and I knew his name was Ezekiel. He touched his finger to his eyebrow and then pointed it at me in greeting. It was funny how he did it, and I laughed in delight.

Then I was in my corner, and I began to wonder how I was to imagine the sheet of light Ahria had told me to employ. But I didn't need to work at imagining it; it was just there, growing outward from our hands until it met in the middle and forming this amazing sheet of light, each corner held securely by each one of the four of us. I began to lower it as Ahria had instructed. "At least 25 feet below the ground" is what she had said. But as I imagined it lowered, I watched it go through the basement but when it got underground, it was so dark, I couldn't see how far it was dropping.

I lost my concentration. And I found myself back where we had started. Taking a deep breath, and breathing it into my being, I calmed myself while the others waited. As I breathed, a knowingness entered with calm and peace, that I should just let the sheet of light slowly fall through the earth until it felt right to allow the process to reverse and to rise with it through the house and eventually to 25 feet above the house - to just go by the feeling of it happening and not directing it, to just ride the wave of light as it moved.

That is what we did. From deep in the earth, I watched the sheet of light as it reversed direction and rose. I saw it go through the basement, through the floor of the first floor. I began to realize that the four of us were also rising at a level just above the sheet of light suspended between us.

When it was about half-way up the flight of stairs between the first and second floor, I began to see and hear what looked like black grease popping and snapping in a very hot frying pan. The grease was black. The frying pan was the brilliant sheet of white light. And that grease popped and spit and bounced as it was cleansed from the air through the action of the sheet of light. The higher we went, the more popping spitting bits accumulated. I knew the black grease-like stuff was the negative energy.

When we reached that point of 25 feet above the house, I watched as we began moving toward each other. My thoughts were wondering how we would tie the ends together, but suddenly when we were about 3 feet apart, the corners of the sheet sucked out of our hands like magnets drawn to each other. Those corners whipped together into a whole, sealing the sheet. We four - Michael, Gabriel, myself, and Ezekiel - released it, lifting our hands to send the bundle up, up and away. Hovering there, 25 feet above my house, I thanked each of them.

Again, Michael winked in farewell, Gabriel bowed, and Ezekiel did the eyebrow thing. They were all grinning at me, and I felt their delight at my acceptance of their presence and at my joy of this moment. They faded away, and I began to slowly descend back into the Labyrinth where my body sat quietly watching all of this.

I relaxed, eyes still closed, marveling at this amazing experience when I heard a dove cooing. Only then did I open my eyes, and looking up, I saw a dove sitting at the very peak of my house. She was cleaning her wing and cooing. When I looked at her, she stopped and looked down at me for a moment. I swear I heard her say in the softest loveliest most confident voice, "It is done."

Then I saw that my house was rimmed in gold, as if a child had taken a crayon made of real gold and outlined the house. But the gold was so bright and so shiny, so full of energy and light that I doubted my eyes. So I closed them, shook my head and looked again. It was still there, that gold outline. I just sat and watched it, and as the sun rose, it slowly began to fade in the light of day. I knew I'd experienced something very special and my excitement had me running into the house to email Ahria to tell her all about it.

I sent the email. I sat there for a moment. I wondered. "Have the prices come down on a flight to California to go to Mt. Shasta?" Since Ahria had left, I had investigated the possibility of taking a trip to Mt. Shasta. Somehow I knew I was supposed to go before June 1. Who knows why? But airline fares and car rentals were just too high. I was still paying off the trip to Findhorn and my frugal nature wasn't allowing me to spend that kind of money. But sitting there that Sunday morning, my urge was to check the fares again. What I pulled up blew my mind!

There was a one hour internet sale where I could get a flight and rent a car for one fourth the cost it had been. I ran over to the Carriage House, woke my mother, told her what I'd found, and she said "GO!" With minutes to spare, I made the reservations. In her pajamas, my mother came in, made some coffee, and sat to hear the story of the cleansing of my house.

I wish I'd had my camera with me that morning, and I wonder if the gold edging of the house would show up in a photograph.

Genesis House and Walking Prayer Labyrinth

<u>Prayers for Protection</u>

At all times, you are completely enfolded within the power, presence and activity of God. You have the faith to proceed forward secure and safe in Divine Love You are protected, not only from any outward negative influence or circumstance, but also from any false inner concerns or old beliefs, Those old beliefs are now being cleansed away. God is your source of inspiration and serenity. Lovingly, faithfully, you affirm your oneness with God and experience the certainty of your protection and security.

The Light of God surrounds you
The Love of God enfolds you.
The Power of God protects you.
The Presence of God watches over you.
Where ever you are, God is
And all is well.

TWENTY

Mt. Shasta

A week later, I was on my way to Mt. Shasta.

Mt. Shasta

My flight took me to Sacramento, where I picked up my rental car and drove the 220 miles to Mt. Shasta, arriving at sundown. The motel room I'd reserved was dreadful - a smoke-free room that reeked of cigarette smoke. After assertive words on my part, I was sent to a motel down the road, which was not much better but at least was smoke free.

First on my agenda the next day was to find a decent place to stay. I went to the Mt. Shasta Visitor's Center where I met a lovely lady who had also been drawn to come there, and now lived in the town of Mt. Shasta. Upon hearing my story, she recommended a place called Alpen-Rose Cottage, a lovely Bed & Breakfast on the outskirts of town. She called the owner, and made arrangements for me to stay there at a fraction of the regular price. I ended up in a wonderful townhouse for $40 a night, with the stipulation that if someone else checked in, I would have to share. Fine with me! As it turned out, I was the only one there for the next four days.

Alpen-Rose Cottage

My first day was spent learning my way around, a bit of grocery shopping, visiting some of the tourist spots, and talking with anyone who was interested in talking. I found the wonderful City Park which holds the head waters of the Sacramento River, a remarkably beautiful spot that I visited for many hours each day.

The second day, I drove up the mountain. My goal was to reach the glacier at about 8,300 foot where folks had reported meeting Saint Germain. The road was pretty steep. At about 7,000 feet, I began feeling a bit strange. At 7,800 feet, I had to pull over at a Vista because the strange feeling was becoming too intense to continue driving. I got out of the car and could barely stand up, let alone walk. A couple, who had also pulled into the Vista site, watched me with concern on their faces. I told them I felt very odd. They offered to drive me down the mountain. I told them I wanted to wait to see if I felt better. I was worried about them driving my rental car because I had signed something swearing I would be the only driver. They made me promise not to try to drive if I still felt badly. I promised, assuring them of my cowardice and my willingness to ask someone if I needed help. They left.

I retrieved my Native American Flute from my rental car, and rather wobbly crossed the road to climb into the forest on the other side, knowing I could go no higher while driving. I found a log to sit upon and I began playing my flute as I waited for the odd feelings in my head and body to subside. The disorientation I was experiencing still has no words to be adequately described.

After a while, I heard a siren coming up the mountain. I saw a police car pull in behind my rental, and the officer got out and looked into my car. Before I could call to him, an ambulance pulled up followed by another vehicle with Fire Chief printed on the side. I guessed that the helpful couple had dialed 911 as soon as their cell phones had service, so I called down to them, "Are you looking for me?"

They saw me and insisted that I stay where I was until they could get to me. The paramedics climbed up to where I sat on the log and practically carried me back down to the ambulance where they hooked me up to oxygen. To make a long story short, I was brought down off the mountain by this trio. The fire chief drove my rental car.

The paramedics told me in answer to my embarrassment at having to be brought down off the mountain, that this happened all the time on Mt. Shasta, and that they would much rather bring me down this way than have to pick up the pieces of my body off the sides of the mountain. They pointed out a burned tree that peeked over the edge of a particularly steep curve. According to the paramedics, someone had misjudged the curve, and their car had landed in that tree. The man had fallen out of it before the car burst into flames and was currently in the hospital recovering from many broken bones.

When we reached the edge of town, a call came in over their radio saying someone had been injured on the glacier, and that broken legs were involved. The trio pulled over into a parking lot, asking if they could leave me there to rest in my car so they could go back up the mountain as quickly as possible. They pointed out the library and said I could wait there until I felt better. As requested, I promised I would call a cab before trying to drive if I still felt bad after an hour or so. After sitting in the car for awhile, I began to feel better and to feel chagrined and dreadfully disappointed at not being able to reach the glacier.

I went into the library, and seeing that internet access was available, I signed up to use their computer. When it was my turn, I opened my email and began composing a letter to my niece Glory, lamenting the fact that I'd spent all this money to come to Mt. Shasta and couldn't even make it up the mountain. "What am I doing here?" I asked in my email. "Why would I be told to come here if I am not able to go all the way up the mountain?" I was close to tears with frustration, and sat there with my fingers on the keys completely bewildered and confused when I heard a voice at the check-out desk that was familiar.

I looked up and saw Jana - Jana from the grocery store at Findhorn - Jana, one of the folks who had told me I was to go to Mt. Shasta.

"JanMarie," she exclaimed. "Oh my God. It was for you. I was told to come here ... for you. What is going on? What has happened?" Then she told me how she had been at an Ashram in India when Spirit told her she was needed in Mt. Shasta. So she came and had arrived only a couple of days previously. She talked of her not knowing why she had to come, not knowing until the moment she saw me. Oddly enough she had received her message the day I bought my airline tickets.

I explained my frustration; I blushed at my having to have been brought off the mountain by paramedics. I whined at the question of being called to Mt. Shasta only to experience this inability to reach the place where St. Germaine had been seen.

Jana laughed in kindness and understanding. "Two things have happened here for you," she said. She explained that what had happened to me on the mountain happens to many people who are sensitive. She assured me that the need for me to come there had been accomplished on a molecular, atomic level telling me that the energy of Mt. Shasta was very special for it is one of the seven most powerful energy vortexes on the earth – an Earth Chakra.

"The reason you became so disoriented is because the mountain was acting on your innermost energy, refining it and tuning it to what it is supposed to be. You would not have experienced this so strongly if it hadn't been so important for you to be here to make these changes. You may never be able to define this change, but know that it has happened, and it is good."

"The second thing that has happened for you," She continued, "is the magic of taking a Leap of Faith. It changes something deep inside of you, which allows you to see and experience even more. It opens a door for you, and as time goes on, you will recognize more and more the changes that have occurred in your own energy field, your own aura."

We talked further, with Jana telling me how she had found a wonderful house to rent for month, but if Spirit called before that month was up, she would go. She shared with me that she felt very strongly that she had been called to answer my questions and my frustration that day in the library.

"Wow!" was my only thought. And to think anything more was a threatening proposition of arrogance and awe. So I left it alone and stepped into my room of gratitude to the powers that be for the help I was receiving. I didn't see Jana again during the remainder of my time at Mt. Shasta.

I spent a lot of time at the City Park, meditating in its beauty and magic. The Bed & Breakfast became a wonderful retreat for me with books to read that seemed written just for me at this point in my life. One book in particular addressed an issue in such a way that I was astonished at its power to be there at the right time and the right place. The issue is too private to detail, but the magic of the synchronicity had to be shared.

I left Mt. Shasta without knowledge of whether I would return. That possibility is still nebulous. Who knows?

Prayers for Guidance

God is your inner source of inspiration. God's loving guidance is always with you. Through the loving Christ presence within, you have the courage and the faith to follow the wisdom of your heart. All things work together to bless you. You are calm and centered. You have a God-given ability to think clearly, to concentrate fully and to express yourself perfectly.

Prayers for General Needs

God knows your needs and assures you that you are worthy and deserving of bountiful goodness. You turn, in trust, to God for the perfect fulfillment of your every need. The Holy Spirit moves in and though your life in powerful ways that harmonize your thoughts and feelings. Your peace of mind, freedom, prosperity, and success are assured.

TWENTY-ONE

What Does It All Mean?

Imagine a thousand piece puzzle spread out all over your dining table. There is no picture on the box lid to give you any clues of what you're constructing. So first you look for the edge pieces to try to get framework. Then perhaps you look for similarity in colors and group those. And if you're lucky, once in a while, you find a couple of pieces - maybe even a dozen that come together.

Until I built the Labyrinth in my front yard, the puzzle of my life had some small parts done - perhaps bits of the edging, and groups of pieces with similar colors. Somehow, meditating and praying in the Labyrinth helped to connect those groupings, and to add to the structure of the edges, but still the picture is not clear.

I do know that I am different than I was before I built the Labyrinth. I feel different. I feel more stable, calmer, more secure, and so much more connected to all that is. I've changed. I can feel it but do not have the words yet to describe what those changes are, what they mean, and where they will lead me next.

Accepting "what is" is easier than it used to be. Living in the *now*, has meaning to me though I still have to work at it. I've learned to listen much better to that *still small voice*[17].

When I retired from teaching, I had left a career where I was very successful, highly respected, and the recipient of various awards - local, state, and national. I'd made my mark in the world, but something was missing. The experiences with the Labyrinth in my front yard have been filled with mystery, with promise, with trepidation, with opportunity, and with an awful lot of questions.

Questions are still there, but they're different now. Before I was searching for God: now I'm searching for ... an unknown quality, an essence, a knowing, an openness that allows me understanding, knowledge and wisdom. I used to think I was not loveable or loved; now it doesn't matter. I find myself more interested in giving love than in receiving it, more comfortable with others, and not so worried about being liked. In some ways, even that is bewildering, for the drama, the angst, the familiar worry has changed. The caring has changed. And letting go became the next lesson.

In December of 2007, I once again came close to death and choosing to live.

In the fall of 2006, I was diagnosed as diabetic and as having sleep apnea - two conditions I suspect were either triggered by the fall on my head in Scotland or a round of Lipitor messing up my body. My research found that diabetes is often caused by Lipitor, and I wondered if the concussions and jarring to my neck, jaw, and head had created the sleep issues. I was still getting used to the sleep machine and diabetes' meds a

---

[17] *The term 'still small voice' comes from the Bible:* **1 Kings 18:20-40; 19:12** *The still small voice was to show Elijah that the work of God need not always be accompanied by dramatic revelation or manifestations.*

year later when I made an unwise choice while getting my dog ready to go for his yearly vet visit.

I was multi-tasking, trying to save myself a trip from house to the car. I put the leash around my right wrist and car keys in my right hand. On the other end of the leash was my feisty, sweet golden/chow mix KuBear. As we came out the back door, I switched my purse also to my right hand as I turned and reached back to pull the door closed with my left hand.

At that moment, as I was facing the door, KuBear saw a squirrel come running past the bottom of the steps. He leapt after it with all the force of his intense strength and energy. My feet did not hit the ground for nearly 10 feet where I landed and rolled in sharp agony. Briefly, according to my surgeon, my shoulder must have dislocated, popped back into place, and all kinds of things were torn.

Surgery was scheduled for December 7, and plans were made to keep me overnight, as I am prone to blood-clots and the doctor wanted to check me over carefully the next morning. Unfortunately, I was in a hospital which had only been open for a few months [one where the CEO had been changed several times already, and one where the nurses were not being allowed to unionize]. Because of this, temporary nurses were being used – nurses who were only there for one or two shifts per month. A patient might have a different nurse each shift and never see that nurse again.

"Nothing to eat or drink after mid-night" and surgery delayed until late into that Friday afternoon left me very thirsty and hungry. It was nearly 8:00 p.m. before I got to my room, where I was helped into the bed and then abandoned. My thirst was overwhelming, so I hit the Call Button, but no one came. Every 20 minutes or so, I hit it again. I could hear it being shut off down at the nurse's station, but no one came.

By 10 p.m., I was miserable and would have cried if I'd had any fluid in my body. After much struggle, I managed to reach my cell-phone in my case that had been left on the bed. They'd given me some kind of shot in the neck to numb me for the surgery, and it was still very strong, so my entire upper right quadrant was almost totally unresponsive to any effort.

I could see my room number on the open door, but had to guess at the hospital phone number. Somehow my guess was accurate and the main switchboard operator answered. I explained to her my predicament, and that no one would come to help me. She connected me to the head nursing supervisor of the hospital.

Within 15 minutes, 3 nurses and a supervisor were there, and I was finally given something to drink. I did not understand how badly dehydrated I was, or I would have asked for an IV to rehydrate myself faster.

In the middle of the night, my legs began to hurt, so I called a nurse. Her response was to tell me to make sure I told the doctor about the leg pain when he came in the next morning. The next morning, a new nurse ignored my complaints about my legs hurting and my concern about possible blood clots. Her answer was that my legs hurt because they put you in funny positions during surgery. Then she left.

When she returned, she told me the doctor had called and that I was to be released. I told her, "No, I am supposed to be checked for blood-clots." She simply said to call my ride to come and get me because the paperwork was done. Still groggy from pain medications which had begun masking the leg pain, I wasn't in much condition to argue further, and before I knew it, I was on my way home in the middle of an ice storm.

Two days later, I awoke with an elephant making itself comfortable on my chest. As the ER doctor put it, "Your lungs are so full of blood clots, there are too many to count."

A day or so later, my minister and two ladies from Unity of Independence Church came to see me in the critical care unit. I was so tired. Breathing was incredibly difficult. Hooked up to all kinds of paraphernalia, I just closed my eyes as the three ladies prayed for me. At that point I was in pretty bad shape and really didn't care if I lived or died. Death actually seemed preferable because breathing was so hard.

At one point, I opened my eyes as Rev. Carla McClellan prayed aloud. Catherine Frink was at the bottom of the bed with her hands on my feet, and Nanci Thomsen was to my left with her hands on my thigh. My eyes opened onto Nanci, and suddenly I saw something seem to course through her body. She jerked, and I felt something enter me - a life giving energy shooting into my body. I knew at that moment that I would live. It felt like something inside me had made a decision, a choice. And once again, the choice was to live.

It was a long journey back to health - another journey leading to living in the NOW[18] - living in the present moment completely. Having to take Warfarin, the rat poison that keeps your blood thin, taught me to take charge of my health and my body. I hated the Warfarin; I hated how it made me feel. I suspected I was having brain bleeds, as there were times I couldn't talk; I couldn't remember simple words like

---

[18] *The phrase 'living in the NOW' comes from Eckhart Tolle's book "The Power of Now" For more information, see: https://www.eckharttolle.com*

"the." I could hear just fine but couldn't understand what people were saying.

I got mad. I went to the Labyrinth to pray for guidance. Then I began to research how to keep my blood thin naturally. I prepared a research paper outlining my diet and supplement plan to keep my blood thin without prescription blood thinners, and I presented it to my cardiologist. He approved it, and I stopped the Warfarin. I've been Warfarin free for several years now, since May of 2008, and I am doing fine.

This was the second time in two years that I had come close to death, and somehow I knew - I just knew - that these two events had been planned by me as a way out of this life - a decision I believed had been made before I'd been born into this body. Both times, I chose to stay. I also *just knew* that I'd accomplished what I had intended for this lifetime, and therefore, anything else was just gravy and completely my choice.

My Choice. My Choice. And I didn't know what I wanted to do. It seemed like every decision of my life up until then was a lame duck decision. I became a teacher because women were not allowed to be Forest Rangers back in the sixties. I hid my art because no one ever encouraged me, and I wasn't sure if it was any good. I did what needed to be done next, day after day after day. Choosing became a chore because I didn't know what I really liked to do. Once again, I went to the Labyrinth to pray, this time, asking "What am I supposed to be doing?"

Prayers for Whatever

The presence of God within you is your peace. From the center of your being, the love of God flows into your life and circumstances, prospering, guiding and harmonizing all that concerns you. You turn your thoughts toward God, and know all things facing you are in divine order. You are free of doubt and concern. You trust that peace, prosperity, guidance, clarity, and wisdom are yours. The perfect fulfillment of your needs unfolds at the right time in your life.

Prayers for Guidance

Through prayer, you are guided to a greater understanding of all that is available, all that is before you, and all that is in Divine Order. The power of the indwelling Christ uplifts and encourages you. Your guidance is clear, and you are inspired to take right action.

Prayers for Healing

The presence of God moves through your body as revitalizing life. There is no obstacle to the free-flowing life of God healing and renewing your body. Every organ and tissue functions in perfect harmony.

TWENTY-TWO

And Other Odd Blessings

When I returned from Findhorn, the visitations of St. Germaine and Jesus during prayer and meditation came with me. John had planted a tree in the center of the Labyrinth, and I'd added a circular wrought iron bench around it. I would go out to walk in prayer and then sit on that bench. When I'd close my eyes, I could see St. Germaine and Jesus sitting on either side of me. Sometimes I'd ask what I should do about something, and often, I'd hear an answer.

John and I were having difficulties, and I began having dreams that he was seeing other women. I've had precognitive dreams in the past and even telepathic dreams at times but they were not usually warnings for me. When they were about others, I'd tried to give cautions to those involved, but the reactions were sometimes very hurtful. A couple of times, those dreams had saved lives, but even these instances were fraught with the peril of losing friendships, which happened several times.

When I began having the dreams about John, I was afraid – afraid to believe them. I'd denied intuition, denied precognition, denied ESP for so long out of fear that it hadn't happened for quite awhile.

In the Labyrinth, when I prayed about the dreams, when I asked Jesus about it, the only thing He would say was "Just love him, and trust the process." So instead of ending the relationship, I would give John another chance. And he would cheat again, and I would first learn about it through dreams. When the dreams came, I would begin snooping, and the evidence was always there. John would never admit it until he knew my evidence was unquestionable. And Jesus continued to say "Just love him, trust the process," and I would try and try and try. Months went by; years passed, and still I prayed.

I became so frustrated, that one day in the labyrinth, when Jesus spoke those words again, I cried out, "What the F**k does that mean?" and Jesus threw back his head and laughed uproariously. I tried until I could not try anymore. And finally I ended the relationship.

This whole process with John became a blessing because I learned to trust my intuition, to trust my dreams, and I learned that I cannot save anyone but myself. I also learned that 'trust' is something completely different than what I thought it was.

I thought trust lived in a realm having to do with what someone else does or what you expect someone else to do. Because of the strange relationship with John, I learned that trust really has to do with trusting yourself to be able to handle something when the events around you are hurtful and difficult.

So what does it all mean? All the synchronicities, all the events, Dorothy's visions, John, St. Germaine, falling on my head, nearly dying a couple of times, and the myriad other stories that I haven't told yet. I wish I could say I've figured it all out but I haven't. I have just learned some things:

1. A higher power does not operate on human time. It took years for me to discover the St. Germaine-Mt. Shasta connections. It took years for me to understand what trust really meant and to learn to trust myself. It took years for all the parts of the puzzle to be presented and to understand that even now, there is still much of the puzzle to complete.

2. Sometimes it's better to not know everything all at once, for struggling to understand may be part of the process of which Jesus spoke. Seeing the process is a lot different than living it. I learn a lot from books - head knowledge, but I learn heart knowledge from living. I consider myself a Liberal Democrat, and I follow Unity principles, but the experience with John's belief system, though incredibly frustrating to me, opened a door of understanding I just didn't have. I thought I could teach John[19] a better way to think, but he just wasn't interested. He was where he was because that is what worked for him. His belief system coupled with his traumatic childhood worked for him.

---

[19] *(Note: John is so much better at some things than I am. He's so much braver; his courage is amazing whereas mine is sometimes non-existent. I cannot state that I am farther along the path than he is, for I could very well be wrong. Just like the Labyrinth fools people into thinking they are far from the goal, when in actuality they are just following their own path.)*

3. Trusting my own intuition and trusting my ability to get through the hard stuff is only a part of the trust issue. I've learned to trust that someone or something is in charge. Whether it is my own higher self, God, the Universe, Spirit Guides, Guardian Angels, or something else indefinable is almost irrelevant to the fact that there is something/someone (inner and/or outer) putting up these signposts - these synchronicities - focusing my attention, and most of all caring about me, where I am going, what I'm doing, and how I'm doing it.

4. My Inner Critic is not going away. It's there needing to be loved, just like all the rest of me. It is not to be pushed away or buried but just understood and appreciated. My discernment, my judgment (both good and bad), my ability to choose wisely, my caution and even my caring all work through my Inner Critic. It is not good or bad, it just is a part of who I am.

5. I learned I do not have to be or to do everything perfectly all the time in order to be loved. I learned this from John. I loved him. When I learned to have compassion for him in his inability to stay true to me or any other woman, I found I could also have compassion for my own failings. And I realized that if I could do that, others could love me too.

6. I learned that the best answers to prayer come when I express what I want in terms that leave room for answers outside my view. For example: putting no stipulations on who comes to fill my lonely house, but

just asking for my house to fill with love and laughter works much better than praying for a particular person to want to come.

7. I've learned that praying in gratitude opens the door to recognizing and appreciating what I already have. When I change my focus from one of need to one of seeing what is already there, I find that all that needed to happen was for me to change my focus.

8. I've learned that when you say you've learned something, the universe presents lots of opportunities for you to prove it.

9. I've learned that your best ideas come when you're preoccupied - in the shower, on the toilet, driving, or anywhere where there is no way to write it down. (I managed to remember #8 as I ran down the stairs with my towel wrapped around me before I could forget that insight.) Perhaps this is why walking a Labyrinth in prayer and meditation works so well: because your body is occupied in doing something else which sets your heart-mind free to hear, to speak, and to know.

10. What I learned the first time I experienced the Labyrinth at All Souls Unitarian Church was just a hint of the years to come, the years between then and now which have been an opportunity to practice learning how to live those epiphanies, and how to make them part of me - including epiphanies about judging myself

and others, epiphanies about my place and the place of others on the path, and epiphanies about letting go, rejoicing in the moments no matter how short or how long, respecting other's needs for solitude, and giving love whether with a touch, a smile, or giving space.

11. I learned how truly connected we all are. From Jana delivering a message in the Findhorn grocery shop, to Barbara seconding that message, and to Ahmed's third. Dorothy, Jack from my church, Ahria, and my date who'd studied Botany - all arriving to deliver messages. Even the young woman who overslept one Findhorn morning and did not come to sand the icy stone walkway upon which I fell onto my head, was an instrument in my journey. Some of those stories are not complete ... I may never know why I had to experience Robyn, but the way my life has gone, I bet someday I will know.

12. I've learned that *learning to live in the mystery* is both the price and the joy in deciding and in choosing to follow Spirit. It entails all of the above, but adds the power of patience to the equation. Time seems non-existent, and all the "shoulds" of life come up to be examined minutely by everyone in your life, including yourself.

13. And finally, I've learned that the *story* has to be told in order to be released. This is about knowing yourself. This is all about knowing yourself, for then, and only then, can you make the changes you desire.

Prayers for Letting Go

I lovingly release my story into the safety of God's gentle care. I know that God's will for me is for my own highest good. My heart is at peace now, as I move forward in my soul's journey.

Life is an eternal process. All life comes from God and all life returns to God. I release my concerns, my fears, my habitual thoughts ... I acknowledge and release my negative thoughts which have plagued me into the loving arms of God, knowing that all of me both perfect and flawed is enfolded and transformed in Divine Love.

I trust in God, knowing that whatever I do, wherever I go, God is the wisdom that guides, the love that blesses, the presence that protects, and the substance that prospers me. I rejoice in the bountiful blessings pouring forth in my life.

Part Four

A New Journey

Introduction

I haven't written anything for months. I've known which part of the story I need to tell next, and I haven't had the discipline, strength or whatever else to make myself do it. Now I know the time is short, and I must finish. Today is April 8, 2014 and I am in Anacortes, Washington to help my Aunt Nona recover from total hip replacement surgery. It is appropriate that I finish the book here, where this part of the story began.

To begin, I only go back a little more than a year. In my home in Missouri, on February 5, 2013, I unplugged the phone, closed the curtains, and did my pre-meditation exercises and breathing regimen as suggested by Edgar Cayce[20]. I even called my brother and asked him not to phone me, as he seems to always call when I am trying to mediate in my chair in the study. It was too cold and wet to walk the Labyrinth, so knowing I was still connected to its powerful energy, I made myself comfortable in my meditation chair.

I was deeply frustrated. Years before, in the Labyrinth, St. Germain and Jesus told me to sell the house, and it has not sold. I'd done everything I could to facilitate that requested sale, but it hadn't happened. As I prepared for meditation, the question of why the house hadn't sold was on my mind. I knew I had to let it go, to let go completely, to just let the question float and try not to think about it. I wanted an answer. I didn't care what the answer was; I just wanted it.

---

[20] *Edgar Cayce, The Sleeping Prophet* For more information, see http://www.edgarcayce.org/

That February day, it wasn't long before I reached an inner and outer state of being that felt like I was both at the Heart of the Universe and at the Heart of Me all at the same time - the ultimate joining of the deepest recesses of the inner me and greatest extension of the outer me. I just *was*, and it was a quiet totality of being I'd never before achieved in meditation.

Floating there, in perfect communion with all there is, I heard a voice, one I'd never heard before or since. It was a magical voice - one full of love and humor, deep and resonate, like a cross between Santa Claus and the one person who loves you completely and totally, like my Grandpa Van. Without any judgment and only love, the voice simply said. "Finish your book." And I knew that the house would not sell until my book was done.

TWENTY-THREE

Sell the House?

Again I have to go back before I can go forward while also staying in the present.

In 2007, while sitting in the middle of my Labyrinth when Jesus told me to sell the house, and St. Germaine added his agreement, I turned to Mary (Jesus' mother) who was also there. Calling upon my team, my Guardian angels, my Spirit Guides, I saw my Great Aunt Helen join us, also nodding in agreement with Mary. "Sell the house."

I argued with them. I pointed out all I'd done to cleanse this house of negative energy, all I'd done to update it physically and spiritually, all it meant to me and to those who came to stay with me. I swept my arm in an arc to indicate this space in my front yard, to my Genesis Labyrinth, which was so important to so many people, and cried, "Why?" I spoke of my plans to turn it into a Retreat Center for Women on the Edge of Change. I reminded them of all the prayer which had so blessed this house.

For months I argued with them. Midst my protests, I did invite a Realtor to come, and she wanted to put it on the market for $239,000. But I just couldn't. I loved the house. I loved the Labyrinth; I loved everything it had come to mean. So I hemmed and hawed, and a year went by ... and the housing market began collapsing.

In 2008, I finally hired a Realtor who said we should ask $210,000. But no one came to look at it, and it did not sell. When his contract was up, I hired another Realtor, who said it had to be under $200,000. Still no one came to look at it so, of course, it did not sell. Another summer came, and I began the process of interviewing Realtors again. I started the practice of interviewing a minimum of five, going into prayer in the Labyrinth before and after each interview.

Each Realtor interviewed asked me the same question, "Why do you want to sell?" I was afraid to tell them that Jesus came to me in my front yard and told me to sell. I didn't want them to think I was nuts, so I'd hem and haw and change the subject. That summer, when Realtor Rick Massie came for his interview, he also asked me the dreaded question. Tired of hemming and hawing, I began making up a story. I lied. Yet was it a lie? Astonishing even to myself, I heard myself lying.

Recently, I had heard of Holos University, both from friends and because my son Adam, who had stopped at the school headquarters near Springfield, Missouri the previous month and spent a day talking with its founder, Norm Shealey. Adam had brought home a catalogue of classes, and though I'd glanced at it, had not thought too much about it. Then Realtor Rick asked his question, and out of my mouth came this story that surprised me with its excitement and passion.

"I want to go back to school," I exclaimed. "To Holos University to learn about Medical Intuition." I jumped up and ran into my den to grab the catalogue. Showing it to Rick, I excitedly told the story of how I'd always had the ability to intuit medical conditions but was afraid to practice it, as I didn't understand the whys and wherefores. I went on and on about how I wanted to go back to school to get my Doctorate, ending my story with the words "Either I'll be 65 with a Doctorate or 65 without one, so I might as well go for it." Realtor Rick was suitably impressed.

After Rick left, I sat there with that catalog in my hand, marveling at my ability to lie to him, as well as being astonished at how excited I had been to tell him about going back to school for this purpose. Astonishing also was my willingness to share with Rick about my medical intuitive abilities because I'd kept that part of me hidden for many years after some very painful "witch" and "of the devil" accusations from one-time friends who had self righteously dumped me.

I thought about that interview with Rick all night and for the next few days. I sat in the Labyrinth praying to understand why I would lie so easily when I worked so hard to always tell the truth. I asked myself if I was listening, especially after hearing the words "Holos University" again only a couple of days later. I shared what had happened with my mother, who now lived in Colorado with my sister Renee, but had just arrived for a visit.

"Call Holos," she said.

"Call them" were also the words I heard in the Labyrinth. So I did, thinking my mother and I might drive down to Norm Shealey's ranch in my motor home to find out about the school. Upon calling, I learned that Holos was moving that Fall to Unity Village, only twelve miles away, and that the Dean of Academics and Dean of Admissions, Ann and Bob Nunley, lived near Lawrence, Kansas., only an hour away. I was given their phone number, so, with my mother's encouragement, I immediately called before I could talk myself out of it.

A couple of days later, my mother and I drove to Lawrence and ended up spending the day with Ann Nunley at her beautiful home on the Kansas prairieland outside Mclouth, Kansas. Before I knew it in that August of 2009, I was signed up and in the process of refinancing the house in order to have the money to pursue my doctorate. So, it was not a lie after all ... just a precognition occurring.

Classes began in September, and as I sat in my Orientation and Planning Class (ORP) listening to the amazing reasons why my classmates had decided to come to school at Holos and what their topic was to be for their doctorate, I was humbled by the honor and nobility of these people. Their goals were truly wonderful, and their desire to help others was inspiring.

A beautiful Native American woman, Ruby, wanted to develop a healing modality for the generations of wounded Native Americans who'd experienced cultural genocide. Another student was studying to develop protocols that would help trauma victims of huge cataclysmic disasters like Katrina and the Indonesian Tsunami. Others wanted to teach nurses in big hospitals how to treat the whole patient - body, mind and spirit. Elisa, who was from Australia, wanted to expand her very successful music career into helping people heal through voice training and sound vibrations.

I listened and applauded, listened and applauded, knowing I was in exalted company and that I had no such goal of comparable value. Ann Nunley, perhaps sensing my silent need, called on me last to share my doctoral goals. Needing desperately to tell the truth both for myself and others, I related the experience with Realtor Rick and how impressed I'd been with the lie I had told him. I laughed as I explained that though it was all a lie, I'd been so impressed with the passion I'd heard coming out of my mouth, that I'd decided to pay attention to it as I'd been praying for guidance in my Walking Prayer Labyrinth as to what I should be doing with my life.

Then the tears came and began to drip down my cheeks. I spoke of how beautiful I found their goals to be, and how embarrassed I was to have to tell them that my doctoral goal came because I knew that I'd be no good to anyone until I was healed – words that surprised even me because they had nothing to do with medical intuition. "I guess you could call my doctorate topic 'Healing JanMarie' I admitted through my tears. I apologized for being so pitiful while at the same time begging for their understanding, as this was something for which I just had to be completely honest.

Holos Provost, Oliver London, was sitting next to me. He leaned toward me and quietly told me that I was being the most honest of all there, saying that if we were to look at the deep inner reason for each of these people to study their particular healing modality, you would find that subconsciously each is seeking their own healing.

Oliver went on to explain that it is common for healers to choose to study and practice healing professions for which they feel the need for themselves. "The difference is that you have already discovered why you are here," he told me, "and they have yet to understand it is their own need they are researching and reaching out to experience." Oliver gave honor to my embarrassed admission, thereby giving me permission to search as I required.

The Indecision Program running through my life at this time is best explained in excerpts from my final paper for this class:

Saving JanMarie

"First you say you do, and then you don't
And then you say you will, and then you won't
You're undecided now
So what are you gonna do?

Now you wanna play, and then it's no
And when you say you'll stay, that's when you go
You're undecided now
So what are you gonna do?"

Made famous in 1951 by the Ames Brothers, this song was being sung by a voice in my head. "Undecided," was published in 1938, so I guess I am not alone in being undecided. About the only thing I have decided, is to take this song "Undecided", which has been playing inside my head and mind for weeks, maybe even months, and begin this paper with it.

The Faces of Indecision

Finding myself in the ORP class of Holos was surprising to me for almost everything I'd found exciting in the past few years seemed to fizzle out after a few hours, a few days, and sometimes even a few weeks. Things that for a moment felt so right, so noble, so within my capacities and interests, raised up like Meringue on a pie, only to be deflated once taken out of the oven, becoming something flat, not interesting anymore, hence losing their effect on my appetite. Everything faded except the desire to know what to do with my life, my purpose, my reason for being - to know anything except this awful indecision.

I took classes, taking what I needed from them, and sometimes not finishing when it came to proving that I had mastered the *material. I took what I needed and left. The Prayer Chaplain training with Silent Unity helped me to learn to pray in the manner I had found so effective when asking for prayer from the Unity Chaplains after various services. However my sensitivity made working for Silent Unity too painful, and I had to quit.*

After hearing Gregg Braden lecture at Unity Village, I started a book club to study his books, but after finishing two, "Divine Matrix" and "Fractals," my interest went elsewhere. Rev. Robin's Sacred Abundance classes took my attention for a while; "Eye of the Storm" classes saw me about half the time; "Zero Limits" and "Ishmael" ended with completion of the books; and the "Course in Miracles" group lasted about a year.

My A.R.E. group is still going quite happily, but then there were a few classes/groups who have been lost in the mists of memory, perhaps because they just weren't memorable. Flitting from one study group to another, from one book to another, from one goal to another, I became lost in the process, so much so that the only thing left to look at was the indecision itself.

The last thing I did that reached inside me and grabbed hold with a surety was to go to Findhorn Garden. I felt a strength to overcome and solve all obstacles. It was the last thing that was so right, so filled with synchronicities. It just took over. It held a knowledge of rightness, incredibly pure and simple.

Feeling that my life had been a life of "shoulds", a life of doing what everyone else thought I should be doing, or rather what I thought I should be doing to fit my current idea of what it meant to be successful - I lost track of my heart's desires in the whole process of trying to be what I thought everyone else wanted me to be. I knew I wanted to change, to grow, to understand, to know who I am. When these entities or spirits or parts of me, showed up at Findhorn, I knew I didn't know what I like., I didn't know what I liked to do. I couldn't think of anything that was mine to do. I knew I just wanted to live a life that didn't hurt so much, that was safe, that was filled with love, friends, and fun. I thought, "if I follow Spirit, I will be safe." I thought, "If I do what Spirit says, I will be living my life right."

My Faces of Indecision are many. I turned to St. Germaine, Jesus, Mary, and even sometimes Joseph to ask what I needed to do. The first thing they told me was to sell my house. So I put it on the market, and no one came to look at it. In more than a year, no one came to look at it. I thought it was a lousy Realtor problem, so I hired a new Realtor, and two people came to look in the second year. The third Realtor was Realtor Rick who was the catalyst for my coming to Holos. In the meantime, no one comes to look at it still, yet my guides continue without fail to tell me to sell the house.

I don't know why. I don't know where I will go, nor what I will do, if and when the house sells. I've gone through the house several times over the years and gotten rid of stuff. That feels good. I've done ceremony several times to facilitate the letting go process within myself. And still, the house does not sell.

The indecision grows and multiplies as this stalemate continues. In prayer, I ask again and again why I must sell; I continue to ask for clarification if it is true that I must sell; I continue to wonder what this is all about; and I continue to be firm in wanting to follow Spirit. Sometimes there are answers, which seem to satisfy for awhile, but then the questioning begins again.

As I learn to 'Trust the process', as directed by Jesus and Mary, I do become more at peace with not knowing. I do find I am coming into touch with something in me that knows I'll be okay no matter what, even though I don't know what it is. Yet at the same time, I am at peace with the indecision, I am also looking at it in a different manner, which a dear friend put into these words for me: "JanMarie, if there is a Spiritual Purpose to this indecision, what do you suppose it could be?"

Prayer for Clarity

The Holy Spirit gently and easily brings to your mind whatever is best for you to do. Your guidance is clear and certain. You are lovingly directed to your highest good. Your way is clear, clarity is yours, and the Christ Light inspires you to take right action.

Prayer for Healing:

The Spirit of God dwells in you and you are filled with life-restoring energy. You release any troubled thought or feeling, and hold to your faith in the face of any challenge. You are healed by the power of the Holy Spirit.

You give your attention to life-affirming ideas and true understanding of who you are. God's healing energy fills your mind. The healing love of God flows through you. Whenever any disturbing thoughts or feelings arise within you, they come to be healed. Thank God for this awareness and that divine love heals you in every way.

Prayers for Selling Property

Divine order surrounds your house and brings a buyer who appreciates its beauty, its value, its worth, and is blessed by its magic. You have faith that God blesses this transaction with promptness, order, and mutual satisfaction. You trust God to guide you to your right destiny. All of your needs are met in a timely and prosperous manner.

TWENTY-FOUR

Holos University

I cried through every class I took at Holos. I wept through every paper I wrote. I willed myself to be honest with myself. I walked the Labyrinth everyday; I prayed for wisdom and guidance. I prayed for strength and resilience. I prayed for the finding of truth and the knowledge of what to do with it, and I cried. I didn't pray for A's but I got them anyway.

Every class was vital to my search. Each classmate was an incredibly blessing in my life - each professor walked my path with me, holding my hand and was present for me every step of the way. Holos professors understand that these studies open long hidden doors inside of each student, so gentleness, understanding, compassion, empathy, and some good healthy pushing is required of them. Holos professors are committed to walking the journey with each student exuding unconditional love and wise discernment.

The day before Thanksgiving that first year, my Inner Counselor professor, Ann Nunley, invited me to come to her home and spend that entire Wednesday with her. Her creation of the Inner Counselor Process many years before had been honed to a marvelous perfection, and had opened doors in me that had been locked for a very long time. But somehow, a door had been opened that was causing me some major issues, so I called Ann and she said, "Come."

For about a month before going to Ann, I had been having episodes where I suddenly felt as if an "abject despair" was dumped over me, as if it were a thick liquid being poured from a giant bucket onto my head. I'd go from a very happy occasion with friends or family, and suddenly while driving home I would become overwhelmed with these feelings of drowning in uncontrollable despair. They were coming faster and more often, and I was getting very frightened.

Ann's Inner Counselor Process helps a person to go back in time to the place where a painful event and resultant emotion or feeling was first experienced. The process facilitator uses their own intuitive skills to recognize when that place has been reached. Often, opportunities come again and again in a lifetime for the subject to resolve those issues, so those intermittent events come up during the process experience.

It is important therefore to make sure the subject gets back to the very first time of occurrence. There, the feeling is faced and transformed in a simple yet dynamic fashion which produces a remarkable healing. This is a very definite process that is guided by the facilitator.

When I went through the process with Ann that day before Thanksgiving, we kept going back and back and back, until I was in another lifetime many centuries ago. When you go through this process, you are there, feeling and seeing it all. It's similar to hypnosis but also very different because you are not hypnotized. It is like watching and being inside of a movie, yet feeling every thought and emotion.

> *I found myself to be a young woman living in a small, stone cottage on the side of a hill. It was very, very green, which makes me think of Ireland or perhaps Scotland. I have two little daughters younger than five years old who are clutching my skirts as we watch the battle that is being waged in the valley below my house. I am frightened both for myself and my little girls. I know that my son in my current life is the reincarnation of one of the girls, and my older sister Jurene is the reincarnation of the other little girl.*
>
> *I also know that no matter who wins the battle, that the men will come. I know they will rape and kill me and my little girls. I have no husband to protect me and nowhere to go. I am in the greatest despair. I take my children into my cottage, and we sit down by the fire. I take them onto my lap and begin to sing to them, withdrawing into my own mind to get away from the coming horror. The despair is like a physical thing smothering me.*

Then Ann led me through the process to transform that event into a place-time-event-experience where it is changed and healed. The most remarkable results were these:

1. I never experienced that despair again.

2. When I got home, my son, who was going through his own despair after the breakup between the mother of his twins and himself, was asleep. He slept for days, and when he woke up, it was evident that something had changed for him ... clarity and healing in him was evident in his face, his talk, in everything about him.

Ann had told us that these past life healings could and often did produce generational healings. If an event in a past life produced severe and profound effects in an individual, their DNA (perhaps Spiritual DNA or perhaps physical DNA?) created that weakness in the descendents of that individual. This means that my withdrawal into my mind and into a fantasy state produced a tendency - DNA-wise - toward that weakness in my descendents. Ann also explained that when that was healed in me, it was also healed generationally and across time, so we could expect to see healings in our lineage.

For my son, this meant that he was able to step away from that withdrawal he'd entered upon the breakup of his partnership. He'd stepped away from the despair. My healing and my son's healing happened just as Ann had predicted in her classes, even though we hadn't considered that my son would be experiencing it, too. My healing of this despair and the tendency it produced in my lineage facilitated the healing for my son.

~~~~~~~~~~~~~~~~~~~~~~

Delphine Rossi was my Sacred Contracts Professor, a class I took at the same time as ORP and Inner Counselor. She and I developed a rapport that was to bring two additional healings for me. Along with teaching Sacred Contracts, Delphine did Past Life Regressions.

At the beginning of the next semester, I drove my motor home to Delphine's home in southern Missouri, and did three regressions which brought answers to three of the biggest questions I'd been carrying throughout my life. Because the incarnation I'd learned about through Ann's Inner Counselor process was so fresh in my mind, I wanted to find out more about this event.

Ms Delphine quickly took me back to that place and time. There she took me to the last day of my life, and had me review what had happened: We had not been raped, and my children had not been killed.

When the warriors had come into my little stone cottage, they had immediately seen that I had lost my mind completely. They saw me singing to my children with strange sounds and words they'd never heard before; they saw my eyes staring into a place they could not see. They were frightened of me, fearing that I was a witch with great powers, and they ran from that cottage. When local villagers came a few days later, I was dying, but my little girls were okay. They were taken in by a childless couple who raised them with love and protection.

Prayers for Spiritual Understanding:

Prayer is a pathway to Spiritual understanding. You see yourself enfolded in love, wisdom and freedom. Through the power of Christ within, you become aware of your spiritual nature. Your heart's desire to know of your oneness with God allows the inner Christ presence incredible power to change your thoughts and actions. You are lifted to greater expressions of God's love.

Prayers for Success in Learning:

You have instant access to the all-knowing mind of God. You rejoice in your God-given faculty of perfect concentration. You think clearly and calmly, you remember what you have learned and you express yourself with confidence. The Spirit of the Lord goes before you and makes your way easy and successful. You are receptive to creative, enriching ideas, memories, and healings. You have faith that God always goes before you, showing you a still more excellent way.

TWENTY-FIVE

Healing Past Lives

When I came into this lifetime, I came with the knowledge of a vitally important moment in my most recent past life. When I was little, I even asked my mother about that memory and she was appalled and tried to get me to forget it. Even today, that memory is still fresh in my mind's eye.

I knew that I had been a child about 7 years old, who along with a little 4-or-5-year-old sister (who is in this lifetime is my older sister, Jurene). We were in the basement of a hospital where Nazi doctors were performing experiments on us. The time I remembered was a day when they had us lined up, wearing sack dresses with our heads shaved and, barefoot on a cold brick floor. They had put my sister onto a table where they were doing something with the blood they were draining out of her.

The nurse who was supposed to be watching my sister began flirting with the doctor. I saw that too much blood was being taken, so it was overflowing the large container and dripping onto the floor. I began to step forward to say something to the nurse. I glanced at my sister. She knew what was happening, and she shook her head. As I stood there, I knew she was asking me to let her die. I stepped back and watched her die.

When the nurse finally looked, she was annoyed and shoved

my sister's body into a trashcan, which was then wheeled away. Then it was my turn. I prayed and prayed she would keep flirting with the doctor so I could die, too. The memory went dark there. I always assumed I had died on that table at the end of that memory, but when Delphine took me back into that lifetime in hypnosis, I discovered I had not died that day.

I lived for another few weeks, until one of the doctors who was experimenting with transplanting animal bones into humans, implanted a baboon's bone into my left foot. This was done with no anesthesia and having experienced several such surgeries, I had learned to "withdraw" into my mind to escape the pain. When the surgery was almost done, soldiers ran into the room screaming that the Americans were coming. Someone picked me up and tossed me into a dark, cold room where several other children were lying on the dirty brick floor. A little girl I'd been trying to help after the loss of my sister crawled to me, and I wrapped my arms around her to try to keep her warm. It was several days before we were found, and I had died from blood loss. [21]

I have had multiple surgeries on my feet in this lifetime, especially the left one. There is a bone spur that keeps growing and breaking, causing a lot of pain.

---

[21] *Note: In the mid 1990's, as an elected delegate to the National Education Association Representative Assembly, a group of us had gone out to dinner with a friend who had recently returned from Russia. He was part of the Jewish delegation that had gone to examine the Nazi records found there. Everyone wanted to know about what they'd found, but before he began, I felt compelled to tell him about my memory of being a Jewish child in the Nazi hospital. He turned pale when he heard my story. He had just returned from Russia, so he knew there was no way I could have known this information. He said my story was exactly the kind of thing they had found that the Nazis were doing, and their delegation was the first to know about it. My memory was confirmed, and his thoughts about reincarnation were probably expanded greatly.*

In 2012, I had surgery again on that foot where a bone had to be shortened because it was too long and causing many problems. During the surgery, the doctor cut himself so many extra precautions had to be made.

One day a couple weeks later, when I was sharing this story about my foot doctor cutting himself, a woman in the group suddenly exclaimed loudly, "He cut himself to let you know that he was the doctor in a past life that operated on your foot and killed you." I did not know this woman, nor did she know me or my past life story. She was as surprised as me at her outburst, and added, "Now where did that come from?" My foot doctor in this life is one of the kindest doctors I know, and has been especially caring about the problems I've had. I took it all as being a reminder to forgive.

In another session that week, Delphine took me to the time just before and during my birth. When I was born, my head was very large hence was badly misshapen from the birth process. My mother often joked that I was 8 pounds head and 2 ounces body. During the hypnosis, I saw myself being handed to my father right after the cord was cut, and hearing him exclaim "Oh, my God. What's wrong with her head? She'll never find a man with a head like that."

I was astonished at this memory, for I thought men did not go into the delivery room in those days. I called my mother that evening and asked her if he had been in the delivery room, and she said that he was there, that he loved babies and always insisted on being present at the birth of his children.

She also affirmed that he had been very upset about my head - that everyone was. His mother spent months gently trying to reshape my head with her hands.

I grew up believing that my father did not love me. My mother always said he did, but I never believed her. I also believed I was unlovable and ugly. Delphine explained that what we hear just before birth and for a time afterwards is taken very literally by the infant, and that as a hypnotist, she was trained to always check those birth moments for issues that needed healing.

In our deep discussion after these hypnosis sessions, I brought up the fact that in all the memories I had of past lives, I had never had a partner, and I had died fairly young in each. Another commonality was that my sister Jurene figured prominently in most of those memories.

One memory not following the storyline exactly for I almost had a partner saw me *on a hill overlooking a harbor where sailing ships rested at anchor. A tall man, a sailor, came to say good-bye to me as he was leaving that day. I looked up into his sky-blue eyes and knew he would not return. I had long black curly hair and wore a brightly colored skirt and peasant blouse. It felt like Greece. We barely knew each other, and I knew I'd already lost him, that his ship would be lost.*

In another memory, I was a young male teen in Kentucky in early colonial days, Jurene was my little sister. Our parents died, and we set out to find people. We got lost in a forest and died of starvation and the elements.

The most detailed memory was of Jurene and I when we were the Jewish daughters of a wealthy farmer (who in this life is my ex-husband, a man who always treated me more like a daughter than a wife) *in Russia during the purging of the Jews by Bolsheviks. Jurene was about 16, and I was about 21 in this incarnation. When our farm was attacked, we escaped and joined a playing troupe which traveled like Gypsies. Jurene was very beautiful and could sing and act. I was very efficient and could cook, sew, repair anything, and manage money. Our goal was to get to America. We were killed crossing the border.*

Another memory, one with a very short partnership, came:

After a very fast courtship (just days) and marriage, my new husband (who I knew as John in this lifetime), *stabbed me to death only hours after we'd married, for no particular reason other than he'd decided he didn't want to be married after all, and all he wanted was my car. He left me on the side of the road, and as I lay dying, I watched him driving off in my car along the dusty road. I was dressed in 1920's fashion, was a very young woman. My clothing as well as the car being mine suggested I had money.* (How odd … in this lifetime, I never feared John. I always knew he would never physically hurt me. Even though he would rage at me, I was never afraid of him … though in that past life I was terrified of him. In this life I also would never let him handle my money.)

I asked Delphine why these early deaths might be. Why was I never partnered? Why was I single in this life? Why didn't men ask me out? Why couldn't I sustain a partnership? Delphine's answer was to be expected: "Let's ask." And she began the process of another regression as I lay on her couch.

I found myself sitting at a dressing table. I knew the year was 1719, and I was a baroness or countess. My maid came into the room to do my hair, and I saw that she was pregnant. Knowing she wasn't married, and being rather self-righteous, I told her she could not work for me any longer, that an unmarried woman who was pregnant was a disgrace. She cried out that the child was my husband's. In a fury, I jumped to my feet and ran from the room.

I knew that my husband had not wanted marital relations from me ever since my miscarriage a year previously from which I almost died. As I ran down the stairs, my fury mounted, and grabbing a horse whip from the stand in the hall, I raced outside, running down the lawns to the road where my husband would soon return. I called him "Flick" for short. We'd grown up together and always loved each other. My name may have been Marie or Margaret or Mary. When I got to the road, I stood there slapping the whip against my skirts where they made a particular sound I can even hear as I write this memory.

When my husband rode up on his horse, I began screaming at him and hitting him with the whip. He grabbed it from me, and told me he would talk to me when I had calmed down. He rode on to the house. My fury grew and grew, and suddenly, I felt something give way inside my head, and I fell to the ground paralyzed. I lay there looking up into the trees above me, knowing in the last few precious seconds that I'd burst a blood vessel in my brain and was dying. I also knew at that moment that he was my soul mate: Saint Germain.

Delphine took me into that place between lives to help me discover the importance of that life. I learned that he had been relieving his sexual needs with my maid out of the fear of getting me pregnant before I was ready. My jealousy had killed me. My anger had killed me. I learned that he loved me completely and had only ridden away to give me time to settle down so he could explain.

I also learned that he has reincarnated into this current lifetime and will be joining me soon. As of 2015, it has not happened. I am still waiting.

Prayers for Inner Peace

Even in the darkest moments of life, God is with you. God loves you and will never forsake you. You keep your focus on the power within you. You linger in this sacred Presence, and you are filled with the peace, love, and understanding that only God can give you. You know that God is in all situations, and you are uplifted. Your mind and heart are open to the possibilities of new hope, new life and new purpose.

Prayers for Love

You gently release any thoughts, feelings, or relationships that no longer serve your highest good. As a radiant being of divine love, you attract a circle of friends to share with, support, and to be supported by. You develop strong, healthy, and loving relationships, and you attract a companion who expresses the attributes and qualities that you desire in a relationship, and you are fulfilled.

TWENTY-SIX

Answers

What I learned through my Holos experience could fill an entire book, but because this is a book about the answers to prayer found through walking the Prayer Labyrinth in my front yard, I will add one more story, the most important healing story that came to fruition through Labyrinth prayer.

I found out why I fell on my head when I went to Findhorn Garden, Scotland. In my class at Holos University on Past Life Hypnotherapy with Morris Netherton, a healing occurred that no one could ever have predicted, and it changed my life unbelievably.

Dr. Morris Netherton is probably the best Past Life Hypnotherapist in the world. [Delphine Rossi is one of his Certified Hynotherpists.] His class was held on Norm Shealey's horse ranch in southern Missouri. For one week, we watched Dr. Netherton work. Each of us was hypnotized in one session, either in the morning or afternoon. Sessions often lasted for three or more hours. Dr. Netherton was searching for people to learn his technique because he is getting close to eighty years old and needing to retire, so we were learning his hypnosis process as well as auditioning to take over for him.

This is Dr. Netherton's story. He remembers a lifetime a thousand years ago in Tibet:

When his parents were dying from influenza, his mother told him to take his little brother, go to the monastery and ask to be adopted into the order. He was 6 or 7 and his brother was about 3. For several days, they knocked at the door of the monastery and were told to go away. Finally, they were allowed to join the monks and begin their training.

After a few months, his little brother started to lament that he was beginning to forget how his mother and father looked. To help the little boy, he began taking him through memory exercises designed to revive those visual memories of their parents. He paid attention as he worked, discovering what was effective and what wasn't, and could soon help his brother to easily bring those memories to life.

The other monks began watching him, seeing how the little brother was helped so beautifully. They began asking him to take them through this process to help them to remember. As the years went by, more and more people came to him for help, and as time went on, these sessions began going into past lives. When he was an old man, he declared, "I am only going to do this for one thousand more years, and then I am done."

Dr. Netherton told us that over the centuries, he continued in different lifetimes to perfect this system culminating in this lifetime. He remembers many of those lifetimes, and has even found records of his work. Now he is looking for those who can carry on the work, for his thousand years is almost done.

Dr. Netherton, on our first day, had given us a form to fill out which required us to list every accident or illness we had ever experienced. I've had a lot of accidents, a lot of surgeries, a lot of illnesses, so my list was long. He told us that HE would choose one of those incidents to be the focus for our personal session. I was the second person to be hypnotized in the class.

It was afternoon. I got comfortable on the matt and cushions on the floor while the class gathered around and Dr. Netherton looked at my list. Then he began.

The only way I can explain what he did is to say that he kept knocking at a door until it opened, then he'd keep knocking until a new door opened, and this went on and on until the final door opened. He did this with words, repeating words and asking me to repeat words I used in answering his questions. From my long list of accidents and illnesses, he chose the fall on my head in Scotland. He took me through that fall, second by second, searching for the second or millesecond that had meaning.

"My head hit the pavement, smack on the back of my head, where the seeing part of my brain is housed … then my legs hit the ground. When I tried to sit up, it was like I was seeing the whole world in a mirror that had shattered and each piece was spinning its own rhythm and rotation. I screamed and covered my eyes. My seeing was all broken, and I was dizzy beyond reason." I said. Dr. Netherton had me tell it again and again, until I was experiencing it completely and thoroughly. He had me repeat certain words over and over again until I used different or additional words, then he'd have me repeat those. And then I said the words "my legs hit the ground," and I added the words, "I could not run".

"Say it again," commanded Dr. Netherton. "Say it again."

"I could not run" "I could not run" "I could not run," I repeated over and over again.

Suddenly, I was back in Anacortes, Washington. I was about five years old and in the house of the child molester who had kidnapped me. I was standing in front of him while he sat on a cot and he had hold of my legs, my bare legs, and <u>I could not run</u>. Dr. Netherton asked me about that day so I told him what I remembered, which was the before and the after: the talking to the man before, and the police rescuing me after. But not the middle, - I didn't remember the middle. I told him about being taken to the hospital and examined, but that the doctor had said the man, though a convicted molester of children, had not appeared to have done anything to me. My bottom looked fine. I told him how much the examination had hurt, and how embarrassed I was with all the strangers watching.

Then Dr. Netherton began taking me through that time until we were moving one milli-second at a time. Over and over and over again, we went through what I remembered until suddenly a door opened in my mind, and I saw what the child molester had done to me. I began to scream. I screamed and screamed and screamed. I coughed and spit copious amounts of mucus, gagging and spitting, and screaming, and screaming … all the while Dr. Netherton encouraging me to spit it out, cough it up and spit it out. I filled a huge 20 gallon basket with wadded-up Kleenex full of mucus.

For hours that day when I was five years old, the child molester had held me against the bar between his kitchen and living room, pounding his penis down my throat, dislocating my jaw over and over again and banging the back of my head against the wall of that bar, hitting my head just where I landed on it in Scotland 53 years later.

When I'd coughed up all I could, Dr. Netherton took me through the experience again, this time telling me to fight back. He held his arm over me to push against. He told me to kick and fight and kick and fight, so I did.

The third time he took me through the experience, he told me to tell the child molester exactly how what he had done had affected my life. I began screaming at him, and what I heard myself say astonished me. Consciously, I'd never known much of what I heard myself say during that hypnosis session. When this happened to me, I was kidnapped about 10 in the morning and rescued about 4 in the afternoon so my dad was at work. He was a lumberjack and was often gone for days at a time. It was summer, so he would be late coming in if he came at all.

When the policeman brought my mother and me back from the hospital, all I wanted to do was pee. I was too little for my feet to reach the floor and I was shaking so badly, I was afraid I'd fall into the toilet, but I could hear my mother talking to the officer. They believed that the molester had not done anything to me because the exam of my bottom (an exam which had hurt terribly) showed nothing, and I couldn't speak when they asked me what he'd done. I'm guessing they thought I was too scared, but now I wonder if I was physically unable to open my mouth as well as unable to describe something I had shut my mind against.

I heard my mother telling the police officer that since I was okay, she did not want my name on any police record because she was afraid of what my dad would do if he found out. She told me when I was an adult that she was afraid my dad would track down the man and kill him, and then "where would we be?" she concluded. I heard the officer agree, saying that since the man had broken his parole, he would go straight back to prison without a trial. (He'd only been out a couple of weeks).

Then I heard my mother telling my sisters that I was okay, and that they were NEVER, EVER to say anything about this ever again. "Daddy must not know," she told them. She made them all promise that they would never tell anyone.

Then she made me promise, too. I just nodded, and inside myself, I thought and began to believe, "I've done something so terrible, it is unspeakable." And I didn't know what it was. I was terrified, and I felt the most miserable shame.

So during that time of the hypnosis, when I was to tell the molester how this affected my life, I screamed, "You destroyed my family. You killed my father. I lost my sisters. I lost my father. I transferred my fear of you to him. I began to believe there was something horribly wrong with me but I didn't know what it was. I was afraid and didn't know why. My sisters became afraid of this secret and looked at me strangely, stepping back from me."

Through my tears, I continued. "My father knew there was a secret, but he couldn't find out what it was. He saw the fear in me and saw me drawing away from him, and he didn't know why. He saw my sisters draw away and hide from him, and he began drinking more and more. He was already an alcoholic, and this tipped him over the edge. Only a few years later, he took a gun and put it to his head and pulled the trigger just outside the door where we six children stood hiding and crying for him to "please stop."

"You destroyed my family. You made me believe my father did not love me. You scared my mother so much she started a secret, a secret she thought would prevent my father from killing the molester and being sent to prison, a secret which murdered our family. You made me believe that if my own father could not love and protect me, then no other man would either ... nor would God." I screamed these last words at the molester and collapsed into heart shredding sobbing.

Then Dr. Netherton had the entire class come and hold me while I cried. They wept with me as they lay down beside me so that every part of my body was being held and hugged tight. I cried and cried until I was spent.

That night, when I went back to my motor home, my throat was terribly sore from all the screaming I'd done. I could taste blood in my mouth, so I took a mirror to look at my throat.

Both of my tonsils were ruptured, the right more than the left. They were split down the middle. I decided I'd better gargle salt water. Gargle, spit, … gargle, spit … gargle, spit … and in the sink, I saw what I absolutely knew was a crystallized pubic hair. Too horrified to move, I watched as it slipped down the drain.

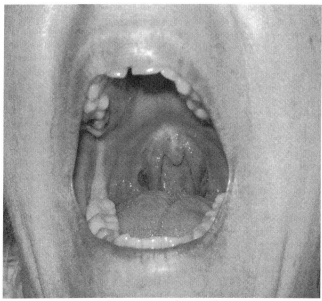

My ruptured tonsils

I called Dr. Netherton and told him what had happened and asked if it was possible for that hair to have been inside my tonsil all that time. He said that in his experience, it happened all too frequently that when a healing occurred, something that had physically been left behind would be released by the body.

When I asked why it hadn't dissolved, he explained that because it was so repugnant to me, my body had walled it off. Then he asked if I'd had a lot of sore throats growing up. I did, terrible sore throats, terrible bouts of strep throat over and over again. Once I'd even missed six weeks of work because of strep throat that wouldn't resolve.

Dr. Netherton explained to the class the next day that the reason he'd continued to encourage me to spit and cough up all that I did was because it was important that the cells of my body remove any vestige of memory of the event. My body produced all that mucus in order to get rid of every atom of semen still in my cells.

The healing that occurred because of Dr. Netherton's work with me was profound. For the first time in my life, things made sense. The PTSD episodes I'd experienced while in training for the "What's the Secret" program of identifying students who've been sexually molested suddenly made sense. My father's death finally made sense. The estrangement from my siblings finally made sense. And with it all, compassion and understanding for everyone concerned bathed me in its embrace.

The fear that I was crazy was gone. I unconsciously stopped chewing my fingernails. The undefined shame was gone. The belief that I was not loveable was gone. The sense of separation no longer hurt me. The anger at my siblings for my perception of being rejected by them was gone. The fear that something terrible was wrong with me was gone.

It's all come full circle. Here I am in Anacortes as I write this chapter, in the library that sits on the land near to where the hospital where I was taken used to be and near where the housing projects were in those days - apartments which had been built to house military families during WWII, and where both my family and the child molester had lived.

Prayer for the Future
You approve of yourself, respect yourself, and treat yourself as the sacred being you are. You appreciate your talents and opportunities. You focus on what you want and practice a lifestyle that expresses your highest nature. As you treat yourself with love and respect, you invite others to treat you with that same love and respect.

Prayer for Forgiveness
No situation or injustice is too great for God's loving forgiveness to heal. You release your concerns into God's tender, loving care, and feel your burdens lifted. You are free, you are whole, and you are at peace.

Prayer for Trust
You trust in God, knowing that whatever you do, wherever you go, God is the wisdom that guides, the love that blesses, the presence that protects, and the substance that prospers you. You rejoice in the bountiful blessings pouring forth in your life.

TWENTY-SEVEN

Why?

For six years, Genesis House has been on the market. In prayer and meditation in the Labyrinth, I have consistently been told to sell the house. Yet after five different Realtors and being on For Sale By Owner, the house has not sold and there have been very few showings.

Why?

The Whys abound. Why am I being told to sell? Why hasn't the house sold? Who's telling me to sell? Why? Why? Why?

The house went on the market again the first week of June 2014, after a year of rest from the stress of always having to be ready for a showing. My fifth Realtor, Jerri Huggins, listening to me ask these whys, listening to me talk about the magic of this property ... with the Genesis Labyrinth, this book, and all that's happened here, made a comment that only this morning registered.

I had been talking about how beautiful the house is, how pleasing it is to me, and how puzzled I am about moving, especially because I do not yet know where I am to go. I remind myself about the lingering balance problems after the fall in Scotland, about the pain in my knees and low back, and how hard the many stairs are on my body. Jerri Huggins, my Realtor, said, "The Magic of this property is you. You are taking it with you; you are not leaving it behind."

****

The ISSEEEM Conference[22] met at Unity Village in May of 2014. Sisters from Wyoming and Michigan sat at my table at dinner one evening. Because they wanted to experience my Labyrinth, they followed me back to my house.

I noticed that night, as I walked the Labyrinth that I didn't feel the energy anymore, yet I prayed as usual, in gratitude, naming the many blessings I have and consciously opening myself to guidance. I wondered if I was so used to the Labyrinth that my ability to sense its energy was lost in familiarity.

The beautiful thought, "The Magic is in me. It goes with me," suddenly came to mind as I walked, and those thoughts were with me when I awoke the next morning. I am not leaving something I will lose; I am taking all the magic with me. This house, this property, this Labyrinth is all now ready for someone else to develop, to grow, and to experience their own magic. This property has served its purpose for me, and it is ready, evolved, and blessed for the future.

****

A couple of weeks after the ISSEEEM Conference, I had just finished mowing the Labyrinth, and had sat down on the bench in the center to meditate. It was dusk, and the street

---

[22] *International Society for the Study of Subtle Energy and Energy Medicine. see http://www.issseem.org/*

lights were about to come on.

As I sat there with my eyes closed, I again asked about selling the house, "Is this what I am supposed to do?" Then I expanded my question to "What am I supposed to be doing right now?"

I listened, and I heard these words "Yes, sell the house" and in answer to my second question, the words came "Get Well." I'd been having trouble with my body not functioning as well as I would like, much pain, balance issues, and awful fatigue. I'd been trying to ignore it. Then and there, I decided it was time to go see a doctor.[23]

As I got quiet again that evening in the Labyrinth, eyes still closed, I noticed that something incredibly light was touching my hands and my arms – exquisitely gentle little touches that came and went. I opened my eyes to find that I was surrounded by hundreds and hundreds of fireflies. I have never seen so many fireflies in one place. They were all around me, some as close as a few inches from my face. I was astonished.

Looking through them to the yards around my property, I saw that there were no fireflies anywhere except in my Labyrinth. I sat and watched them for several minutes, transfixed by this amazing sight.

As they began to slowly disperse, I heard a voice that drew my attention to the sidewalk where a young man was standing. He called my name in an excited tone, exclaiming,

---

[23] *A Rheumatologist diagnosed the problem as a bad flare of Fibromyalgia, I did several rounds of physical therapy in water, very warm salt water. TaiChi in water turned out to be the best treatment for me. With the help of my OB-GYN, I also lost more than 30 pounds.*

"JanMarie, have I told you the new Bible verse I have memorized?" I do not know how he knew my name as I certainly did not know him.

Just imagine me sitting under the tree with the young man standing on the sidewalk. Then add hundreds and hundreds of fireflies.

Not waiting for an answer, he began to recite this verse from memory, John 14:3:

"In My Father's house are many mansions; if it were not so, I would have told you; for I go to prepare a place for you. If I go and prepare a place for you, I will come again and receive you to Myself, that where I am, there you may be also. And you know the way where I am going."

The fireflies and the very excited young man disappeared as I was lost in wonder and realizing how they had brought wonderful answers as I sat in the Walking Prayer Labyrinth in my Front Yard.

Misty, barely there, rising for review now and then, an idea whispers to me. Edgar Cayce always said, "Mind is the Builder." Myrtle and Charles Fillmore, the founders of Unity School of Practical Christianity also taught this precept. What we think, intentions we express, and ideas have the opportunity to become REALITY in this physical world.

Once again, this idea whispering had surrounded me as I prepared for a new tenant in the Carriage House. The idea I was noticing was that all the intentions I've prayed about in the Labyrinth have almost all been realized, perhaps not exactly as I envisioned, but they did happen. The latest is this: I often thought whenever it was time to find a new tenant that having a gay man as a tenant would be a very good thing. He would be helpful and non-threatening, fun and thoughtful, and would keep a neat attractive home. All these years, I've had mostly women as tenants, and excepting one, had good experiences. I did fear getting someone who was a liar, porn obsessed, and/or an alcoholic. I had one who was the exception. I got what I feared all in one person, but mostly I got what I hoped for in tenants.

Another thing I wished for was to have Unity people living here, perhaps ministerial students. The tenants who are moving out because they've bought a house, are wonderful, highly respected Unity people, both employees of Unity Village as well as being associated on a high level with Holos University. Another tenant was a Unity ministerial student. And my next tenant is a gay Unity ministerial student who is excited to live here and work at Silent Unity as he takes classes leading up to enrolling in Unity Ministerial School.

Over the years, I prayed for a partner, a soul mate, knowing that soul mates are those people who come into your life with whom you have a very strong connection and with whom you grow and learn in powerful ways. My prayers in the Labyrinth brought John. That relationship lasted as long as it was supposed to last to give me the opportunities to learn to love unconditionally both me and him.

One of the things I had considered for this property was to open a Retreat Center for Women or Men on the Edge of Change. I've thought on one level that I never accomplished that intention, but on another level, I realize that I did. Both men and women came to stay for awhile during those transition periods in their lives: my nieces, Glory, Wendy, and even Audria: for short periods, my brother Rory: my son: my sister Renee whenever she needed space to rest: my grandniece and nephews, Phelicity, Austin, Noah; and, of course, Garrett with his sisters, Cherie, Megan, and Aubrey. Rachel, Susie, Bernadette, Linda, and many other women who came here to study uplifting books in small groups were engaged in spiritual transformation of one sort or another.

Then there was Beder, the son of Saudi Arabia's equivalent to our Director of the FBI, who was here during the horror of 911, a young man terrified of those events who needed a strong hand to encourage him and to teach him to take care of himself, a young man who had always had servants to tend to his needs. And most fun of all, a young man from China working on his Doctorate in studies of Harry Truman delighted us all with his intelligence, humor, and struggle with the English language. All were in times of change in their lives, so I did accomplish that goal of having a Retreat Center, even though it was not a business but rather a heart connection experience.

Another intention I'd had for decades was to write a book, yet didn't know what it should be about. Here I am writing a book. I wanted to do something with my art and my poetry

... I began creating inspirational greeting cards with my own poetry, calling them Genesis House Creations. When I was invited to the White House, I was told not to bring a gift for President Clinton as it would just go to charity. However, his Social Secretary, Sarah Farnsworth was so wonderful to me, a little nobody second grade teacher, that I did a watercolor of the White House with a poem on it honoring her work for the President. She liked it so much she hung it in her office, giving me the intense joy of being able to say "I had a painting hanging in the White House!"

Another intention with this property was to have a place for family to come to visit. And they did. Not all of them came, but many did. Being in the center of the country, I was an easy stopping place for family going from here to there. They all knew they were welcome, so felt free to call at the last minute to stop by for a few hours, days, or even weeks at a time, another intention realized.

How blessed I have been living here. How blessed to have so many intentions brought to fruition. The healings that happened here, the epiphanies, the blessings, the friendships, the connections, and all the miraculous events have made Genesis House Walking Prayer Labyrinth rather amazing. So I ask again, *WHY* am I told in prayer to sell? Where am I going from here? What is it that is mine to do?

Intention can be a two-edged sword, though we don't think of it in relation to careless thinking and even more careless words. My fear of admitting to people that the reason this property is for sale is because I want to follow Spirit, hence the voice I hear in prayer telling me to sell is the true reason this property is for sale. The trouble is, the mystery of it all is overwhelming at times. I want to know why. I don't like not knowing. It feels like a vacuum waiting to be filled with meaning. Therefore, I fall into the trap of guessing, and thoughts become unconscious prayers.

This is hard to admit, but I am wondering if this flare of Fibromyalgia is being caused by my careless words that the house is too much for me anymore, that the stairs are too much for my knees, that taking care of this big property was more than I can handle. In order to prove my words, did the Universe arrange for this flare of pain, stiffness, weakness, and awful fatigue? The warm water therapy worked very well, but I know I must watch my thoughts carefully to make sure I don't send myself into a place and time I truly do not want.

Every thought is a prayer; every thought is an intention. Coupled with the powerful energy of the Labyrinth, those thoughts reach fruition faster and faster in my life.

With that statement comes an incredible recognition and remembering. Was it a precognition before going to Scotland, or was it a fearful thought being manifested that had me worried on my journey that I would not be liked or accepted? Which of these was the cause of the Robyn reaction? What other careless thoughts wait to manifest in my life?

Prayers for Me

Make me a blessing, Lord! Help me
To help those needing help, to be
A blessing to my fellow men.
Instruct me when to speak and when
To hold my speech, when to be bold
In giving and when to withhold;
And if I have not strength enough,
Then give me strength, Lord, make me tough
With my own self but tender toward
All others. Let there be outpoured
On me the gentleness to bless
All who have need of gentleness.
Give me a word, a touch to fill
The lonely life, faith for the ill,
And courage to keep hearts up though
My own is feeling just as slow.
When men have bitter things to meet
And quail and would accept defeat,
Then let me lift their eyes to see
The vision of Thy victory.
Help me to help; help me to give
The wisdom ad the will to live!

By James Dillet Freeman[24]

---

[24] *htttps://en.wikipedia.org/wiki/James_Dillet_Freeman*

TWENTY-EIGHT

Every Thought is a Prayer

This is a book about recognizing the answers to prayer, about answers to prayer brought through walking in the Labyrinth in my front yard, about learning how to pray, learning how to listen, and learning how to see. It's a book about many of the prayer methodologies I experienced for myself as well as through witnessing the stories and prayers of others, how the answers to prayers appeared or seemed absent ... how prayer answers could be common, strange, inspiring, scary, expected, unexpected, unexplainable, and sometimes even bizarre.

This book is also about the processes we may experience when we pray. Some prayers were answered almost before they were uttered, others took years and years and years to be answered, and others are still waiting for completion. Again, it's all part of the process. And it is about the evolution of a person's prayer life, how it changes and grows, how needs change and grow, and how prayer requests change and grow.

On Easter Sunday of 2014, being in Anacortes, WA, out of simple nostalgia, I attended the church where I had my first communion. Though I do not consider myself to be Catholic anymore, I went to St. Mary's. As I listened to the congregation praying, I realized I needed to write a bit about what prayer is and has been for me.

When the congregation began to pray: "Lord have mercy, Christ have mercy, Lord have mercy, Pray for us sinners, Hear our prayer", I bristled. When I was taught to pray like that as a child, inside of myself, I heard "I am bad. All I can do is beg for mercy. There is no other avenue of redemption for I am a sinner and bad, bad, bad. I have no control. I have no power. The people I love have no power for they are sinners, too. So, please God, please, please, please, love me, too. Please Mary, love me, too. Tell Jesus to tell God to love me, too."

This kind of prayer beat me down, filled me with guilt, until I believed I wasn't worthy of anything good. I believed that way for a very long time. Children believe what they are told by people they perceive to be in control, the boss, the authority, and I believed what I was told.

I've learned that prayer is not answered by some giant bearded man on a throne up in the sky, though sometimes when I pray, you would think I was talking to that benevolent judgmental fellow. This is not a book about God; this is a book about Prayer. So if God is a fellow sitting on a throne, my apologies.

Some realms of thought say that prayer does not change the outside world, that prayer only changes the person who is praying ... by changing how a person views the problem, thus expanding their awareness into being open to opportunity. Others point out that prayer changes how a person feels about the problem, changes how a person experiences an event, and changes how a person reacts to the participants in the problem thereby opening the door to answers. I suspect prayer is a bit about all of these.

When I began walking my Labyrinth, I didn't really know how to pray. Raised Catholic and excommunicated when I divorced, I had gone to many different churches searching for God. I studied various religions, took lots of classes, learned to meditate, and searched for God.

I tried all kinds of prayer. Here's my own list:
1. Begging prayers ... *Please God, make my daddy stop yelling.*
2. Bargaining prayer .... *God, if you will make my dad stop hitting my mom, I will go to church every day.*
3. Pity or Guilt prayer ... *Have mercy on me a sinner, an undeserving sinner, just have mercy, please, please, please love me, too.*
4. Rote prayer ... *5 Hail Mary's and 2 Lord's Prayer*
5. Scripture prayer ... *"The Lord is my Shepherd..."*
6. Gratitude Prayer ...*Thank you God for bringing me:...*
7. Talking Prayer ... *Hey God, how's it going. I'm having some trouble with .....*
8. Pretending to Pray ... *I'll pretend You are real and pray just in case."*
9. The Rosary or Prayer Beads *(Another form of rote prayer that actually works rather well to calm a too-busy mind)*
10. Ho'oponopono ... *"I love you. I'm sorry. Please forgive me. Thank you."*
11. Affirmative Prayer [25]... *As a child of God, you are blessed ..."*

---

[25] *Affirmative Prayer examples are written at the end of each chapter.*

Through the Association for Research and Enlightenment, the home base for the Edgar Cayce readings, I have been a member of the Search for God Study Group for many years. I still use their suggestions for Meditation, their physical exercises and breathing techniques. [26]

The evolution of prayer in my life led me to Unity. In the late 1800's, Myrtle Fillmore was dying from a disease of the time called consumption (we know it as Tuberculosis) . She was given about six months to live. She began the process of teaching herself to believe that she would be healed. She first acknowledged the diagnosis, and then she changed it by teaching herself through words like this: "I am a child of God, and as a child of God, I do not inherit illness."

Affirming her status as a beloved child of God, she reached that place of complete belief, and therefore changed the process going on in her body from one of illness to one of health. She lived into her nineties. She and her husband founded Unity, the School of Practical Christianity in Lee's Summit, Missouri, where I now attend services at Unity Village Chapel. [27]

At the end of each chapter, I wrote an affirmative prayer which addresses something in that chapter. This method of using affirmative prayers was taught to me when I trained to be a Prayer Chaplain for Unity, and again when I was trained to work for Silent Unity,[28] the most powerful prayer ministry serving the public in today's world. Silent Unity is open 24/7 with more than 130 affirmative prayer chaplains ready to pray

---

[26] http://www.edgarcayce.org/are/spiritualGrowth.aspx?id=2874

[27] *http://www.unityvillagechapel.org/*

[28] *1-800-NOW-PRAY will take you to the Prayer Line*

with whoever calls.

Unity taught me Affirmative Prayer, and as you have read throughout this book, these prayers train the mind to think in terms of worthiness, of value, of opportunity, of possibility, and of ability to receive the answers being sought.

Ho'oponopono is an extremely powerful prayer modality. Joe Vitale writes of this process in his book "Zero Limits."[29] Even though this type of prayer has worked amazingly well in my life, these incidents involve others whose privacy I value very highly, so I must suggest you learn of its use on your own.

The prayers on my list are all prayers I have prayed. None of them were wrong, and all of them were right. They were where I was, and where I may again someday be. All prayer is reaching for God. You reach from where you are. I used to think that I would only get the answers if I phrased my prayer perfectly. I knew I was wearing blinders consisting of many different things, so I worried that my prayers would not be answered. Here are some of those issues many people experience when praying:

1. Fear: undefined, ill-conceived, unreasoned fear
2. Feelings of unworthiness
3. Expectations of specific results
4. Insecurity about being able to see the answers
5. Not knowing the how, when, or why to trust when the "still small voice" speaks.
6. Not knowing how to recognize answer to prayer
7. Disbelief in your right or worthiness for an answer
8. Ill-defined desires
9. Refusal to understand that thoughts are prayers

---

[29] *http://www.zerolimits.info/*

I believe all the answers are always there. It is our own issues that hide them, and sometimes it is the process of learning to recognize the answer that is the important lesson. Being raised to believe I was a sinner is a concept that had to be healed. The affirmative prayers spoken over and over and over again served to facilitate that healing. They were so powerful in that respect, I chose to end each chapter with Affirmative Prayers. They opened the doors to being able to hear the answers, for if you cannot believe you are worthy, you will not hear any answers.

I completely believe God wants what is best for each of us and that we each are truly loved. It took a long time for me to get to that point. The Labyrinth helped me learn to listen, to clarify and to recognize what I needed to do, where I needed to go, and to develop the faith and trust that I am indeed loved. Learning to recognize the answers when they come has been and is, an on-going process.

I have come to believe that "The universe rearranges itself around our states of consciousness." [30]

Genesis Walking Prayer Labyrinth in my front yard was and is a tool. Because a part of our brain/mind must focus on walking, turning, and following the path, the praying part of our mind is better able to concentrate on a healthy way to think about the object of the prayer. Once reaching the center, it is time to listen. There were times when my mind could calm enough to listen, and there were those times I continued walking and walking and walking until my mind was finally able to still.

---

[30] *From* <u>*Twelve Conditions of a Miracle*</u> *by Todd Micheal*

This process of getting to the stillness has worked incredibly well for others as well as me, as evidenced in the stories in this book. Teaching my mind how to think to bring about what I want as opposed to what I fear was a very powerful lesson I learned - in often painful ways - through the Labyrinth walking ... and is an on-going lesson as well.

The understanding that every thought is a prayer is still something I have to constantly discipline myself to maintain. Prayer trains the mind how to accept the good that is waiting to speak through from the stillness.

Learning to live in the mystery, to trust, to have faith, to enjoy the adventure, to revel in the process, and to let go of the fear are all components to the power of prayer. They are also the secret to getting to the answers, to being open to the answers, to being able to hear the answers however they may show up, and to being able to step out hand in hand with Spirit to live a blessed life.

This is not a book about the scientific reasons why walking a prayer Labyrinth works so well. I believe all answers to all of our prayers and questions are right in front of us all the time. Somehow walking the Labyrinth helps us to see, hear, and figure out those answers in a very powerful way.

Because the Labyrinth Effect is so very powerful, it must be treated with intelligence, respect, openness, discernment, wisdom, and compassion both for self and for others.

And so it is ... Namaste`

Prayers for Spiritual Understanding

Prayer is a pathway to greater spiritual understanding. You enfold yourself in God's love and light. You know (he/she) is growing in love, wisdom and freedom. You are uplifted and inspired – ready to experience the great and wonderful possibilities open to you now.

Prayers for Protection

With each breath, we release all our concerns and rest in an awareness of divine protection. God is in this situation of mystery. Nothing can challenge the power of God's love to bless you and keep you safe. God within is your courage and confidence to move forward.

Prayers for the Sale of one Home and Buying Another

Divine Order governs the universe and Divine Order governs your life. Your property is surrounded by God's love, and all transactions concerning it are prompt, orderly and mutually satisfying. You trust God to guide you to your right place. Your needs are met and you are at peace.

Made in the USA
Columbia, SC
15 August 2017